Value and Voice
Solutions to Organizational Gender Balance

Second Edition

David Rowell

Value and Voice: Solutions to Organizational Gender Balance

Copyright © 2018, 2019 by David Rowell. All rights reserved.

No part of this publication may be reproduced, stored in a retrieval system or transmitted in any way by any means, electronic, mechanical, photocopy, recording or otherwise without the prior permission of the author except for a brief quotation in a book review.

This book is designed to provide accurate and authoritative information about the subject matter covered. This information is given with the understanding that neither the author nor Parity Press is engaged in rendering legal, professional advice. Since the details of your situation are fact dependent, you should additionally seek the services of a competent professional.

Published by Parity Press

First Printing, 2019

Published in the United States of America

ISBN: 978-1727419276

www.paritycf.com

Dedication

First and foremost, this book is dedicated to all the gender champions out there whose tireless work in areas important to many have made positive impacts in the lives of women and men across the globe. I have meet so many of you in this community, and those encounters has been some of the most rewarding of my career.

This book is also dedicated to all the undervalued who have fought for value and voice; each is truly worthy of all of support, championing, and admiration.

I wish also to note my appreciation for much of my child-rearing at the hands of two very confident and vocal grandmothers, who, though long passed, might have been seen as ideal strong women in their time.

And the biggest thank-you is for my wife, Sarah, not only for her continued patience and too often underappreciated support of with my work, but also for her unwavering strength and values making me a better me.

Contents

Preface	vi
Chapter 1: Disparity	1
Chapter 2: Gendered Traits	22
Chapter 3: Imbalance	38
Chapter 4: Gender Balance	54
Chapter 5: Awareness	68
Chapter 6: Safety	80
Chapter 7: Inclusion	96
Chapter 8: Inclusion of Gendered Traits	111
Chapter 9: Allies	123
Chapter 10: Authority	139
Chapter 11: Empowerment	149
Chapter 12: Balance by the Numbers	168
Conclusion	179
Notes	183
About the Author	187

Preface

This is the second edition of this book, which comes more quickly on the heels of edition 1 than most books. My interest in putting out this new edition so soon is one largely of passion for this topic—that same passion that led to me to perhaps rush the first edition. Having shared this information in even more forums as of late, I determined a bit of reorganization would be helpful in ensuring solutions stand out a bit more clearly. And in that process, new and important material has been added.

I wish I could say that an update was necessary to keep current with trends and statistics. Sadly, however, that is not the case. Gender balance issues have largely remained unchanged, despite even more national and international attention than was present when the first edition was written.

It can still be said that the overall inequality between men and women continues largely unabated.

Not long ago a World Economic Forum report said, "equality is in retreat. For the first time since the group began tracking the issue in 2006, years of global gains made by women are beginning to erode. The current forecast is that it could take anywhere from 83 to 100 years to close the gender gap." The head of education, gender, and work at the World Economic Forum said, "In 2017, we should not be seeing progress towards gender parity shift into reverse."

Another large segment of the discourse has been female participation in science, technology, engineering, and math (STEM) fields, and this discourse is muddled. One might take away from all the chatter that women are advancing across the board, especially in STEM. Yet in some sectors that is far from the case. For example, women are earning bachelor's degrees in computer science at an ever shrinking rate; down from approximately 38% of awarded degrees in 1987 to about 23% in 2015.[1] And the Society of Women Engineers states that "The number of women in engineering in the U.S. has not increased since the early 2000s."[2] Such facts paint a picture that may not be so rosy after all.

And, of course, blatant sexual harassment cannot be overlooked. Sexual harassment continues to be a big topic in public air space because it continues to be a real issue in the workplace. A whole chapter of this book has been dedicated to this topic in this updated edition.

These facts support the continued existence of inequality and imbalance and perhaps also paint a bleak forecast. Women still face and are harmed by a variety of additional inequalities. These include undervaluation, disempowerment, biases, outright discrimination, and even more wrongful, egregious, and wicked harms.

On the other hand, there are some clear signs of progress as well as ever increasing awareness of the issues. There are some indicators of closing wage gaps in Western developed countries, for example. And a good many organizations are voluntarily adding women's voices and contributions at all levels. Some governments are doing the same. In fact, some countries, such as Norway and Spain, have enacted laws that prescribe balanced executive leadership. Regulations that require that no more than 60% of a public corporation's board be made up of one gender. Likewise, some countries—India, for example—have new laws requiring certain numbers when it comes to elections and public representation. Furthermore, in regard to overall awareness, sexual harassment has received a lot of press lately. The media is frequently airing stories about sexual harassment, such as #MeToo and Harvey Weinstein. More importantly, an outcome of this attention is that a large number of sexual harassers are getting their just due.

Despite the prominence of dialog, not everyone sees the issue the same way or shares interest in addressing the issues. There is active debate about the fight for and continued need for gender equality. It's not about whether or not gender inequality exists, but rather one of taking a position on magnitude and pervasiveness. Here is the largest area of disagreement. The disagreement over magnitude and pervasiveness within organizations skews opinion on what to do now—if anything.

One reason for varying perspectives is that people may look at different indicators. Or it may be the indicators are misinterpreted, misunderstood, or unacknowledged. A final factor is quite simply that the indicators are not all numbers-bound. Rather, they can be far less tangible and harder to quantify. This is an important point. Not only do the issues of gender equality need to be qualified to find real solutions, but they need to be qualified even in the absence of quantification. Furthermore, the solutions themselves cannot be numbers-bound. It is important to acknowledge that fact in order to not to oversimplify the problem or limit the solutions.

Before explaining further, let me take a step or two back.

For many years, the book *Start with Why* by Simon Sinek has been in the "Must Read" column of the recommended reading list I share with workshop participants. The premise is simple and powerful: people won't act unless they see the reason for doing so. Throughout the whole of my career as an instructor I began introductions with that principle in mind: giving students the why before the what. I ardently believe that we must be given reason to invest time or effort into anything. I am also enough of a realist to understand that oftentimes people simply need to know what's in it for them. When it comes to the greater of human motivations, altruistic rational wins the day.

It should be pointed out that men can be disadvantaged in certain imbalanced situations. *Gender* is not itself synonymous with *female*. And justice is not—or should not be—bounded by gender any more than justice should be bounded by race, socioeconomics, or any other discrimination category. This book focuses much attention on the inequalities women are subjected to and ways to remedy them, but that does not mean inequality is a female-only issue or a female-only concern.

I will go a step further and say that not only is gender equality a mutual concern, but most of the solutions are mutual as well. The ideal of gender equality is that everyone benefits mutually. Togetherness and cooperation are required to reach that ideal. Men and women not only need to see the issues the same way, but they must also address them in collaboration. This is especially true in the workplace.

It is important to understand that while wrongful and gender-discriminatory behaviors injure individuals, especially and egregiously so women, there is also injury to employing organizations.

As evidence of organizational benefit, consider this for starters:

- A 2007 Catalyst study found a correlation between women's representation on S&P 500 companies' boards and a significantly higher return on equity, a higher return on sales, and a higher return on invested capital.[3]

- A *Harvard Business Review* article said that increasing the number of women in the C-suite from 0% to 30% results in a one percentage point increase in net margin.[4] That translates into a 15% increase in profitability for a typical firm.

- A Credit Suisse press release in 2012 said that companies with at least one woman on their board had a higher return on investment than companies with no women on their board.[5]

Study after study supports direct ties between balance and organizational benefit. Organizations that excel at empowering women correspondingly excel on a number of performance indicators.

The fact is that the more women who are in and empowered in an organization, the more success the organization has. And the more gender-balanced an organization is, the better it performs. I would think men and women alike would want to be part of organizations that purposely work to that end.

Allow me to backtrack a bit.

General Tommy Franks, who led the US forces in the liberation of Kuwait, said, "I, for one, begin with intent."

Establishing connection with students and achieving buy-in to the content of instruction is imperative for successful knowledge transfer. As an instructor, I begin each workshop, class, or presentation by addressing the *why* with intent statements. Declaration of intent does several things: it creates context, sets appropriate expectations, connects with people intellectually and emotionally, engenders involvement, encourages reciprocity, shows respect, and more. What I most hope it does is set the appropriate expectations and engender involvement. I see intent in this circumstance as a contract between the reader and the author as a promise to deliver if you are willing to receive.

My intent is to:

- Define and identify forms of imbalance and their bases to further your understanding of gender issues.
- Identify ramifications of imbalance to encourage some personal action to the benefit of self and/or others.
- Identify solutions to imbalance and the actions necessary to achieve them.

In this book I also plan to frame all of this based on my experiences. That experience includes being a leadership, team-building, and diversity instructor for about 15 years in the federal government. Perhaps more relevant is my work as a national diversity chair, the leader of a federal gender focus group, and a member of a UN organization's panel of experts on gender mainstreaming.

Based on my experience and knowledge, this book thus focuses on workplace disparities, their hurtful results, and solutions to address them.

This book will define workplace gender imbalance and identify its forms. Numbers (e.g., male/female staffing and representation ratios) certainly do represent a relevant form of imbalance, and it would be an untenable oversight to omit that discussion. The numbers (recruiting, retention, and ratios) can be a fix to a host of imbalance issues, but they are only one issue and one solution. Largely for that reason, numeric representation is not the thrust of this book. Balance in this book does not mean numbers equality. Rather, I propose that real balance comes in the form of effect rather than condition: men and women having equitable experiences, especially in the workplace. Most importantly, *parity* will be (re)defined in terms of three things: (1) contribution parity, (2) influence parity, and (3) resulting experiential parity.

To get to balance a number of things must be made clear. To start with, there must be an understanding that any solution suggested here is not gender-exclusive—both men and women have a stake and a role. We'll discuss how organizations can help women, how women can help themselves, how women can help other women, and how men can help women. Then perhaps the hardest pill to swallow is how helping women improves conditions for both men and women. Ultimately, gender balance yields a better experience for both men and women, so the effort is truly mutually beneficial and the behaviors mutually empowering.

Men must be part of the process of women's empowerment. It's not that women can't or shouldn't fend for themselves. It is not a matter of capability or optics or rightfulness. Rather, men are needed as a matter of expediency. Men and women working together is the most efficient means to the end.

I have personally been questioned whether can I assist in female empowerment without the experiential understanding of being female. It is a legitimate question, but there are also are multiple legitimate answers. Rather than reciting my credentials, please consider this: many men are in positions of power and not only may be able to directly assist women, but also may have insider information that is highly beneficial to women, especially those not privy to it.

A colleague of mine, Jeffery Tobias Halter of YWomen, recently gave me another reason. He said to me, "If nothing else, it can be of great benefit to women to hear a male perspective."

Male privilege is not necessarily a bad thing. For one thing, it comes with influence. I have always worked to use my male privilege and my advantage of voice to be heard in this battle. Where opportunities have presented themselves, I have made use of it. In doing so, however, it has never been my intent, nor is it my intent here, to in any way mansplain female empowerment. I will, however, share what I have learned by working the issue at national and international levels. I will ask that you accept me as an ally to the cause of gender balance, gender parity, female empowerment, feminism, or however you care to tag it.

I want this book to be a resource and benefit to both women and men. You will find here recommendations for helping both women and men.

I hope both men and women will read this book and perhaps even read it together, or at least discuss its content.

I hope an investment of your time here will not only result in furthering your knowledge and understanding of these topics but also cause you to take action. I want us all to make a difference. I hope you will find ways to further empower yourself and others to the betterment of women and men and to cause positive change in the workplace.

My message is a simple one that is entirely aligned with my beliefs and who I am: Gender imbalance is everywhere, and everywhere includes the workplace in particular. Gender imbalance is wrong. It can and should be improved upon to the betterment of individuals and organizations alike.

I struggled mightily when I first decided I wanted to write a book on this topic. My passion and intent were strong, but I was concerned about doing the topic justice, even given my experience. I reached out to a mentor, who reminded me to practice what I preach. While my workshops always have lessons in the power of authenticity, my mentor had to remind me how important it is to operate from my core and, in this case, to write and teach from self.

Here I will also make a confession of bias in the interest of full disclosure. When I say imbalance is everywhere, I'll say it's also right in my own backyard. My wife is in a male-dominated career—she is a university band director. In fact, according to the 2011 College Music Society directory, only 9% of university band directors in the United States are women. Those few women conductors in this field struggle with being considered competent or worthy enough to fulfill what is sometimes presumed to be a male role, as well as with the male-centric environment itself. And I have seen these struggles literally very close to—er, at home.

This personal experience adds to a plethora of professional experience as a diversity and gender specialist with the US government, as well as gender work with a UN organization.

I do feel extremely fortunate to have been able to do the work that is true to me. I have often wondered how many people are so lucky to do work that truly resonates with them. I hope that is the case with you and that this book plays a part in helping you progress along your proper path.

People of passion are not rare, in my experience. I would not assume in any case that my passion is enough to warrant your time. But I hope I have established adequate intent, adequate credibility, and an adequate initial case for the need of and benefits of gender balance to go forward.

Chapter 1

Disparity

If you were to do an online search on the topic of gender in the workforce, you would likely come across a number of stories about improvements for women. You would likely see statistics that are touted as positives for women, an upward trend. For example, you might learn that women own close to 10 million businesses.

Such indicators foster the perspective that equality is always advancing. But of course, there is ample evidence that this is not the case. While improvement is happening in some places, it is not happening everywhere, and in some places it is slipping.

According to the World Economic Forum, "equality is in retreat." For the first time since the group started tracking the issue, years of global gains made by women are beginning to erode.

Numerous indicators support the position of retreating equality. Aside from a male–female pay gap, leadership representation gets the most attention.

- Only 28.5% of key management personnel positions were held by women in 2015–2016.[6]

- Globally, women represented only 15% of board members in 2015–2016.[7] In the US in 2016 there was an increase in the percentage of firms with no women in senior management, 33% compared to 32% last year.[8]

- Women make up nearly 44% of the federal workforce, yet they comprise only about 30% of senior executive service positions. Women hold about 38% of GS-14 and GS-15 positions.[9]

Imbalance remains.

However, the focus of this book is not numerical indicators, such as leadership representation. In fact, balance here will not be defined by representation. Rather, we'll look beyond numerical representation to actual impact. I will focus on the causes and effects of imbalance as well as how to mitigate the determinants of those effects. A strong case will be made throughout this book that disparity is detrimental to any organization and very harmful to individuals. But there are solutions that benefit organizations and individuals alike, and the solutions are not numbers-bound.

Let's begin with bias.

Bias

Consider the assumption that gender bias always disfavors women at the hands of men. It is true that women are subjected to more harmful discrimination, both in amount and type, but men can also be so subjected.

Bias is directed at both men and women.

A 2016 *Harvard Business Review* article noted that 70% of men felt a little discriminated against, and 30% said they've experienced at least moderate discrimination. And did you know that the average CEO height in the US is 6'3", while the average male height is 5'10". In the US, short men are targets of discrimination. Discrimination is often tied to perceived virile masculinity, and value is derived from that. As a result, you will see more men discriminated against for exhibiting or possessing feminine traits, for example, especially in male-dominated workplaces and professions. This will be discussed in more detail as we progress.

I am fairly certain that the pain of male discrimination is no less acute for a man than female discrimination is for a woman. Discrimination is personal for all who are recipients of it.

Bias is perpetuated by both men and women in near equal amounts.

Yale research in 2012 found that both male and female hiring officials were equally guilty of gender bias.[10] Another study showed that female professors were just as biased against women students as their male colleagues were. In another, both men and women gave women lower scores in exerting leadership, assertiveness, value for revenue generation, and seriousness about career. Likewise, another survey found that 60.8% of male technical workers and 60.4% of female technical workers indicated their male managers had high technical skills, while only 40.5% of male technical workers and 35.4% of female technical workers indicated their female managers had high technical skills. Both sexes rated their male managers much higher than their female managers. And female managers account for just over 23% of negative critical feedback in written reviews of other women.[11] That may seem small; however, in the cited study the women surveyed wrote only 25% of the reviews looked at to begin with, thus the amount of critical feedback given is commensurate to that as given by men.

Implicit Bias

How much discrimination is conscious versus unconscious bias is debatable. Unconscious bias, also known as implicit bias or implicit social cognition, has received a deserved measure of attention as of late. Unconscious bias refers to the attitudes or stereotypes that affect our understanding, actions, and decisions in an unconscious manner.

These biases, which encompass both favorable and unfavorable assessments, are activated involuntarily and without an individual's awareness or intentional control.

The implicit associations we harbor in our subconscious cause us to have feelings and attitudes about other people based on characteristics such as race, ethnicity, age, and appearance. These associations develop over the course of a lifetime, beginning at a very early age through exposure to direct and indirect messages. In addition to early life experiences, the media and news programming are often-cited origins of implicit associations.

Implicit biases are pervasive. Everyone holds unconscious beliefs about various social and identity groups, one such being gender. Everyone possesses bias, even people with avowed commitments to impartiality, such as judges.

These biases reside deep in the subconscious and are not accessible through introspection.

We generally tend to hold implicit biases that favor our own ingroup, though research has shown that we can still hold implicit biases against our ingroup.

Unconscious bias is far more prevalent than conscious prejudice and is also often incompatible with one's conscious values. Certain scenarios can activate unconscious attitudes and beliefs. For example, biases may be more prevalent when multitasking or working under time pressure. Unconscious biases run unchecked in workplaces of imbalance.

Female Exclusive Bias and Discrimination
Despite the source of bias, it can be said with certainty that more discrimination is directed at women. This in no small part due to the fact that most organizations are imbalanced male.

In the average company, a woman is 18% less likely to be promoted than a man.[12]

Women are nearly twice as likely as men to say they have experienced gender discrimination in the workplace. Forty-two percent of US women say they've experienced some type of discrimination on the job because of their gender, and 25% say they earn less than a man doing the exact same job according to a 2017 Pew Research study.[13]

In 2016 Fairygodboss and Artemis Connection released a survey that identified the workplace challenges that are unique to or have a greater impact on women.[14] These included (in order, with greatest impact at the top of the list):

- Overall feelings of inclusion
- Work/life balance
- Childcare
- Mentorship
- Compensation
- Promotion timeliness
- Harassment
- Flexible work options

The fact is that women do face more obstacles than men—and especially so in imbalanced workplaces. The vast majority are obstacles that men will never endure, even where they are a minority.

Some handicaps uniquely apply to women. Research conducted by Joan C. Williams identified four (maternal wall, tightrope bias, prove it again, tug-of-war, and isolation),[15] and I have added a few others:

- **Maternal wall:** The maternal wall represents the stereotypes and various forms of discrimination encountered by working mothers and mothers seeking employment.Motherhood is commonly seen as a liability and detriment. It is also common that female staff with children are seen more as mothers than as professionals and leaders. This is role incongruence, in which women are often related to as wives, daughters, or caregivers rather than as professional colleagues. Mothers and potential mothers are devalued as lesser professionals.

- **Tightrope bias (aka the double bind):** Women walk a perilous path between being too masculine and too feminine. Women have to choose between being seen as competent (masculine) or likeable (feminine). Successful women are rated as less likable than men, and average women are rated as less competent than men. Female leaders are expected to be collaborative, caring, and helpful rather than to exhibit such typically masculine traits as decisiveness and assertiveness. If a woman acts like a leader, she violates the gender stereotype. If she acts like a woman, she violates the leadership stereotype. When women act like men, they no longer fit the socially expected ideals of women. This is huge issue in male-dominated environments because women feel they must set aside authenticity and conform by being one of the guys in order to succeed.

- **Prove It Again:** Women in the workplace, especially male-dominated ones, have to demonstrate their worth over and over. In fact, a woman needs to be 2.5 times more productive than a man to receive the same acknowledgment of accomplishment. It is as if men are given a 500-piece puzzle to complete, while women have to work with 1,250 pieces. Being average is seen as falling behind. Women are not automatically granted credibility, something that is often the case with men. Rather, women must earn credibility by exceeding expectations numerous times. In a 2018 *60 Minutes* piece, it was reported that women at DuPont were promoted every 30 to 36 months into the same kinds of jobs men were promoted into every 18 to 24 months.

- **Tug-of-war:** This can lead to woman-on-woman sabotage. In male-dominated workplaces, women often pit themselves against each other (particularly intergenerationally) rather than help each other. The more unbalanced the workplace, the more women bully each other. Part of the reason is the perception that the pie is limited—thinking that only so many women will be promoted in a given cycle, for example. More often than not, those perceptions are ungrounded and erroneous, but in sexist organizations, there may be truth to the perception. In either case, the behaviors are further amplified by favoritism threat, which is discrimination against women who help other women. Favoritism threat causes women to avoid helping other women solely as means to be seen as one of the in group, one of the guys.

- **Isolation:** This is an obvious and direct effect of being a minority. In most places it is simply hard for women to connect with men, let alone crash through the "good old boys' club." Even where the numbers may be more balanced, women may self-isolate because they may not want to appear to take sides. Women are judged more harshly across the board and thus can be seen as *sucking up* to the males in power. Or in understanding that women are devalued, they may feel it us in their own interest to separate themselves from other women. All of this results in a unique situation for women, whereby the advantages of connections are known, but can't be taken advantage of for fear of pejorative assumption and judgment. Isolation greatly hampers effectiveness.

- **Stolen voice:** Men interrupt women more than they interrupt men and more than women interrupt men. Women are silenced or their voices are lessened in a number of ways. *Bropropriating* happens when a male steals an idea from a woman and puts it into the world as his own. Bropropriating was used in a satirical International FedEx commercial that gained a lot of attention. Likewise, there is *hepeating* in which a male says something a female just said and takes credit for it himself. *Manterrupting* occurs when a man interrupts a woman, especially excessively. *Mansplaining* is when a man explains something to a woman in a condescending way when he either doesn't know anything about it or knows far less than the woman he is talking to.

- **Expendability:** Women are often expected to do workplace housework (clean, organize parties), and women are disproportionately asked to serve on committees. Women are often given impossible tasks or put on teams with no future. Whereas men are assigned or asked to do something, women are "given a chance" that often sets them up for failure. Often the situation is already known to be impossible. Women often fall on swords. Other times a woman may fail as a matter of self-fulling prophecy. Confirmation bias is inserted when the chance-giver "just knows" the woman will fail.

- **Domestic distractions:** According to the US Bureau of Labor Statistics, women spend one to two times more than men do on domestic responsibilities every day. These home responsibilities consume a large number of hours at work. And they consume a lot of energy that could be better spent being work productive. There is change taking place, where men are increasingly picking up and more domestic responsibilities, but as statistics show this is still by and large a women's burden.

Here's a litmus test: imagine a man being subjected to any of these. Most likely, you cannot.

These purely gender-related obstacles may appear to be handicaps that personally affect women, but keep in mind they also directly or indirectly affect the organization's ability to perform, produce, and serve.

There is also bias related to attire in many professions, and this arguably also a women-only bias. My wife is a band director and conductor at a top-tier university. I can tell you firsthand that there are various gender issues in that imbalanced environment, including attire. Podium attire is such a big deal that it even warrants workshops on how to dress for the podium specific to women at national music conferences. A dissertation by a colleague of my wife's included this as a key piece of evidence of the ways being a band director was gendered.

Here are some excerpts (condensed and minus citations) from that dissertation.[16]

- Women conductors have reported struggling with keeping the focus on the music and not on them. Some strive for keeping their femininity intact visually while feeling compelled to "adopt a surrogate masculinity."

- Conductor Marietta Nien-hwa Cheng speaks to this issue, revealing making a conscious effort to always wear slacks in rehearsal, because "pants offer more authority and attract less attention to gender." For performances, conductors who identify as male often don a traditional formal tuxedo. When a conductor who identifies as a woman decides to wear a tuxedo to conduct, her intent may be simply to emulate the visual standard of the position with the hope that attention is paid to the music and not the outfit.

- This is another example of devaluing women who conduct: first we notice and then we judge what she is wearing, before the first beat of music begins.

- A role comes with expectations. Included within that expectation is that the conductor may wear clothing that represents such authority. Here is where women conductors face expectations in ways that men do not. For men, there is an established uniform: a tuxedo, usually with tails. For women, there is no standard uniform—a woman conductor's body comprises a primary focus to the audience and the musicians.

The reason I didn't include attire as a female-only bias is that men too can be judged, harangued, and disempowered for attire. In the case of men it is often for dressing too feminine. When men cross gender lines in attire, they too can face consequences. It may even be argued that when it comes to attire, that women actually have more leeway in choice of gendered expression. Still, in preparing to go to the classroom, the office, or the work site, it is women who have to consider their attire choices each and every day, who look in the mirror in the morning and question how they might be judged, what standard do they need to conform to, and so on.

The real issue here is that clothing—specifically masculine clothing—is tied to power, to which women have more restricted access. The power resides with masculine dress as both as a product of patriarchy and as a product of being the minority. Regardless of source, it bolsters our case concerning imbalance. Where one sex has sanctioned use of power attire, be it a tuxedo or suit and tie, what is the effect on contributions from and influence of the other sex? Attire can represent visible credibility and authority.

Of course, power is not exclusive to clothing. Consider the ways power is tied to methodologies, speaking patterns, visible gestures and behaviors, and so on. Then ask yourself which sex gets to set the standard and thus benefit more from those standards.

Sexism

The biggest scourge of all, and often the gorilla in the room, is sexism. I trust I don't have to argue the evils of sexism, but I might point out that bias and sexism are far more prevalent in imbalanced organizations. If we are talking about personal implications of disparity, this gorilla is 10 feet tall and weighs 2,000 pounds.

Whether it's in government, academia, law, retail, manufacturing, tech, food service, or any other area where the workplace is unbalanced, discrimination is a by-product. Sexism manifests in many forms, overt and subtle.

The subtle forms may include when a man interrupts a woman who is talking, benevolent offers of help to women employees when no help is needed, or a woman being asked to take notes in a meeting when it's not her job. While such sexist behaviors may be less conspicuous, they are no less unfair, restricting, or condescending.

The more overt—and still very prominent—forms sexism that get more attention:

- **Hiring:** Women are hired less often and paid less throughout their careers. Studies (the National Bureau of Economic Research, for example) conclude changing a male name on an application to a female name greatly affects the odds of being hired. When identical applications were graded, "John" got an average of 4 while "Jennifer" received a 3.3.

- **Pay:** When women are hired in science, for example, their starting salaries are on average nearly $4,000 lower than men's (female applicants $26,507.94; male applicants $30,238.10). On average, female scientists earn just 82% of what male scientists earn in the United States. The difference is even greater in Europe. Female corporate managers earn 68% of male wages, female doctors earn 77% of male wages, female financial managers earn 68% of male wages, and female low-wage workers (e.g., retail) earn 64% of male wages. Overall, women in the United States working full time in 2015 earned approximately 80 cents on the dollar compared to men.

- **Performance ratings:** Standards and evaluations are not equal. Despite identical performance ratings for men and women, more men are promoted. In December 2017 the *New York Post* reported on a Palatine Analytics study that found that female applicants were rated significantly lower than men in competence, hireability, and whether the scientist would be willing to mentor the student. Sixty-six percent of women's performance reviews in the tech industry contained negative personality feedback, such as "You could be less judgmental." That compares to only 1% of men's reviews. The study discovered that women provided almost identical performance review scores to men and women, while 70% of men provided higher evaluations to men than to women. This disparity was more pronounced in senior positions, where approximately 75% of men provided higher reviews to men than to women. A recent AI-powered study found that men and women were equally likely to meet goals in the workplace but that men were getting 25% more positive evaluations compared to women in the same role.

- **Letters of recommendation:** Female scientists are less likely to receive glowing letters of recommendation when applying for postdoctoral fellowships (15% of female applicants vs. 80% of male applicants). Across the breadth of professional fields, letters of recommendation for women populated with grindstone words, words that may attest to good hard work but not necessarily to standout work. Letters of recommendation for men are peppered with standout words that suggest the work is above and beyond. Sample standout words used to describe men were *excellent, superb, outstanding, magnificent, unique, exceptional, extraordinary, unparalleled, amazing, most, supremely, unmatched*. Sample standout words used to describe women were *hardworking, conscientious, dependable, meticulous, methodical, thorough, industrious, diligent, busy, dedicated, careful, persistent, reliable, organized*.

- **Feedback:** Here again the story is more of the same: women are 1.4 times more likely to receive critical subjective feedback.[17] Also, 58.9% of the reviews received by men contained critical feedback. 87.9% of the reviews received by women did.[18]

You can clearly see disparity with the examples above. These are both perceptions and direct impacts.

Additional more subtle comparative impacts often include:

Men	Women
Weighed on potential	Weighed on performance
Performance overestimated	Performance underrecognized and underacknowledged
Mistakes are noticed less	Mistakes are noticed more
Skill	Luck
Benefit of the doubt	Held to objective standard
Given credit for successful outcomes	Blamed for failures
Increased credit for others' ideas	The stolen idea
Masculine traits valued more	Feminine traits valued less

Often these things are a matter of degree and at times they are very subtle. Yet even small slights have big effects. For example, a 1% bias (e.g., 1% lower evaluations) against any group results in 15% lower representation at the upper levels of an organization.

And sometimes the bias has huge ramifications. Ahead of the 2016 election, my mother said to me, "I could never vote for Hillary. I just don't think a woman can be president." In her defense (albeit a weak defense), she is a product of her times. Still, I couldn't just let the comment go, so I pressed her and asked why not. She responded, "I don't see how a woman could lead the country like leading troops into war." That is the crux of the matter in many cases of bias: the key word *see*. It is about opening eyes to possibilities and exposure to images that serve as models of the position. Can't *see* women as firefighters, can't *see* a woman captaining a vessel, can't *see* women leading troops, can't *see* women traveling often, can't *see* a female CFO, can't *see* women entertaining foreign businessmen, and so on.

Stereotypes

One of the reasons people "can't see" is because stereotypes block the view. Female stereotypes are often a direct fallout of sexism. Stereotypes are more pronounced in imbalanced organizations. Stereotypes are more commonly directed at women than at men. And stereotypes judge women far more critically and far more often than men.

A recent study from Indiana University found that gender stereotypes about women's ability in mathematics negatively affect their performance.[19] Because of stereotypes women themselves can't see themselves doing well at math. Interestingly, the study also found that both men and women believed those same stereotypes would actually motivate women to perform better. That is not true.

Where stereotyping is present, stereotype threat is also present.

In experiencing stereotype threat, people in the minority group feel stress when they go against the stereotypes associated with that group. This causes the target of the stereotype threat to underperform. For example, consider the stereotypes directed at women concerning mathematical ability. A woman may do poorly on a math test solely because she fears she will. Anxiety about stereotypes sometimes causes even greater stereotypical behavior as self-fulfilling prophecy, in a sense. Studies show the effect is even more pronounced when people are reminded of their gender before any activity. And women are subjected to many reminders of their gender, especially so where they are a minority or disempowered.

Likewise, stereotypes can cause role incongruence (e.g., women related to as wives, daughters, or caregivers rather than as professional colleagues), which results in conflicts and barriers.

Stereotypes may be used to undermine the ability of both men and women to perform non-stereotypical tasks and behaviors. When the sole representative of a group is a token, that person tries to live up to the stereotypes even more.

Ability itself can also be modulated by the suggestion that the ability is tied to a stereotypical gender function, for example, mental rotation. If it is said that an ability is used in engineering, men excel at it. If you tell a woman it's used in interior design, her ability automatically increases. Gendered behaviors can be primed for both sexes in a number of ways. When people are shown photographs of other people in other roles (e.g., doctor, police officer) and then asked to list their own traits, they often note and exhibit traits commonly associated with the picture they recently saw. Role models are thus also an issue in imbalanced organizations.

Confirmation Bias

A related concept is confirmation bias, whereby biases (and stereotypes) are looked for and confirmed. If you tell a group of students, for example, to look around the room for the color red, the students will find many more red objects than they will if you tell them to look for objects of various colors. Likewise, if a person suspects a specific attribute exists among a group or even in a specific person, odds are the attribute will be found. When it comes to gender, men notice and remember more incompetence in women in confirmation of preexisting bias. A number of other biases and stereotypes are likewise confirmed.

Confirmation bias is not limited to women, however. Men can also be tagged with suspected stereotypical traits, especially in imbalanced organizations. Consider, for example, confirmation bias of a male leader being uncaring and the resulting ramifications. Or that a man in a female-dominated profession is effeminate. Such unjustified devaluation has both personal and organizational effects.

Gender Traits: Stereotypes, Bias, and Devaluation

I now give you stereotype/bias/prejudice (prejudgment) exhibit A:

Leadership and Masculinity/Femininity

Characteristic	Leadership Trait	Masculine Trait	Feminine Trait
Achiever	74%	94%	6%
Aggressive	83%	99%	1%
Analytical	61%	61%	39%
Caring	35%	1%	99%
Confident	100%	97%	3%
Dynamic	65%	77%	33%
Deferential	17%	1%	99%
Devious	0%	74%	26%
Intuitive	87%	15%	85%
Loving	9%	4%	96%
Manipulative	13%	85%	15%
Nurturing	13%	1%	99%
Organized	91%	15%	85%
Passive	0%	0%	100%
A Planner	87%	33%	67%
Powerful	70%	98%	2%
Sensitive	17%	3%	97%
Strong	83%	96%	4%
Relationship-oriented	30%	4%	96%
Rule Oriented	30%	90%	10%
Total: Direct Correlations with Leadership		7	3
Total: Inverse Correlations with Leadership		3	7

I have used this chart in both leadership and gender discussions, and I always point out three things. First, this is a poll that was conducted by a small East Coast university. It is not scientific research. And thus, as a public poll, it is largely a matter of personal opinion and simply individual perception. But understand that perception for any person is their reality. Second, the poll included equal numbers of male and female respondents. Thus, these views are equally held by a good number of men and a good number of women. Third, the listed traits are labeled masculine and feminine and not male and female. As masculine and feminine gender traits, assuming they are even properly classified to begin with, they could be practiced by either sex.

We will take a closer look at gender traits in a later chapter, but for now the most important thing to point out is that there are more masculine traits than feminine traits that are associated with (prejudged as) as leadership traits, even though reality suggests otherwise. A 2008 McKinsey & Company study found that organizational performance is reinforced by nine leadership behaviors, five of which women more frequently apply than men, and thus directly contribute to organizational success.[20]

This poll is no outlier. In classes, workshops, studies, and elsewhere, when people are asked to draw a leader, the vast majority still draw a man.

In 2019 *masculine* and *leader* are still synonymous with and generally assumed to be male.

I always suggest when I present the chart that I wish I had a whole day to address it alone. There are a number of subtle and yet complex and insidious things that lie underneath what seems a simple chart of data rendering of perception.

Consider, for example, that the column labels are *masculine* and *feminine*. While there is some appropriateness here, as will be discussed later, there is also a problem: despite these labels, many read them as *male* and *female*. I can't say for sure that those taking the poll saw it that way, but I can tell you that in my workshops this is always the initial assumption by most participants. Masculine is considered male, and feminine considered female—at least in reflex. When given consideration, many recognize this as not an absolute.

Another problem is in grouping. In circular fashion it is both the basis of and the outcome of stereotyping. When we say men are like this and women are like that, the grouping causes separation and isolation. There is great willingness on the part of some men and women to ensure separation of masculinity and femininity and, to a degree, of men from women. Even in more egalitarian settings, you may hear the term *female boss*. A woman who fights fires is a *female firefighter*. And a man who is a nurse is a *male nurse*. Not only does this binary distinction have the effect of segregating men from women, but it also creates a view whereby masculine and feminine are seen as competing opposite forces that are weighed and measured against each other, and in turn men and women.

Oppositional Sexism

This then brings us to another form of sexism quite detrimental to workplace performance: oppositional sexism.

Oppositional sexism legitimizes feminine expression in women and delegitimizes feminine expression in men (and vice versa for masculinity).

Oppositional sexism makes more difficult the very thing needed in today's organizations: utilization of cross-gender skills. Binary gender views are the biggest hurdle in embracing and using the full suite of leverageable traits that could be well employed in the workplace.

Oppositional sexism plays no favorites. It can be said to impede men and women equally. And it can both acerbate imbalance and be acerbated by imbalance.

As product of a binary gender system, one that strongly adheres to the notion that men and women are opposite, many hold strong beliefs that all women should be feminine and all men masculine. Biases toward people of either sex is based primarily on a sense of what is right or wrong for men and what is right or wrong for women. Likeability is one example: it is considered right for women and thus is expected.

Whether or not we see ourselves as rigid or liberal in this regard, most of us have very firm ideas when it comes to gender. We might not admit it, but most people have a personal concept of gender appropriateness. And our gender-appropriate views are not left in our cars in the parking lot; they walk right onto the factory floor or into our cubicles and offices, and they remain with us throughout the workday.

We typically don't give these things a lot of thought, especially during the course of a busy workday. But we all have preset gender boundaries that are wide or restrictive. Women who do not fit our ideals of femininity and men who do not fit our ideals of masculinity may raise eyebrows, cause mistrust, or impede working relationships. Both women and men can actually feel *threatened* when gender lines are crossed. Such incursions impinge upon personal beliefs and/or somehow threaten one's own sex. Those who venture too far beyond the stipulated borders are marginalized, stigmatized, ostracized, and subordinated.

Consider what happens when a woman strikes a pointedly aggressive posture or a man shows too much emotion. Those examples are only the tips of many icebergs.

Ramifications to perceived incursions are more common with women. When women take on positions typically held by men, they encounter varying forms of discrimination and stereotypical behavior by men and women alike.[21] When women stray too far into men's domain to the point they assimilate behaviors such as being direct, they can be overtly criticized and tagged with derogatory terms such *bitchy* because such behavior runs counter to how women are "supposed" to act.

We can abdicate some of the responsibility by blaming conditioning. There are a number of sources for these beliefs, and they are largely the result of socialization. In the family, at school, in the workplace, in places of worship, and through the media, people receive messages about what male and female should be. We are *taught* oppositional sexism.

A nursery rhyme asks what little boys and little girls are made of. The answer is:

> Slugs and snails
> And puppy-dogs' tails,
> That's what little boys are made of.
> Sugar and spice
> And everything nice,
> That's what little girls are made of.

The adult version? *Men Are from Mars, Women Are from Venus* by John Gray.

Oppositional sexism has ugly siblings: *heterosexism*, which could be said to be a twin in that the beliefs are largely the same as oppositional sexism in regard to male/female appropriateness, and *stereotype inversion*, whereby masculinity has more negative connotations when applied to women (e.g., bold, direct), and femininity has more negative connotations when applied to men (e.g., insecure, shy, weak).

These things are behaviors just as much beliefs. Attitudes and behaviors are linked. Thus, when someone appears to be contradictory to the belief, oppositional sexism results in marginalizing or discriminatory behavior toward that person. For example, men who appear reserved or tentative are tagged as wishy-washy, soft, or a pansy and subject to separation, isolation, or discrimination. Likewise, women who express traits typically associated with men—being aggressive or insensitive, for example—are often judged harshly, scorned, excluded, and held up publicly as bad example.

Oppositional sexism thus functions as a box of legitimacy.

The societal correctness for women includes being nurturing, pious, pure, submissive, domestic, friendly, warm, and nice.

Women who are nice earn less in the workplace.

The female box extends into the workplace, where women are expected to be cooperative, deferential, and conforming. Female domestic expectations cause women to be tagged time and time again as the birthday and retirement celebration organizers. These expectations of female traits and behaviors bump heads with the expectations of leaders to be commanding, for example.

For women it is an ongoing battle between gendered expectations and varying workplace expectations.

Earlier, I described this as a tightrope, and it is also known as a double bind. Women must walk a perilous path between being too masculine and too feminine. Women can be, and are encouraged to be, strong but not masculine, for example. Many women feel they have to jettison femininity to fit into androcentric workplace cultures. They may assume masculine behaviors while distancing themselves from feminine qualities in order to blend in and/or be seen as acting like one of the guys. Some women may even feel compelled to hide specific details about their personal lives, such as children or pregnancy.

Other women feel inclined to take a different approach. They may actually avoid anything that may make them appear masculine because they know women who act like men no longer fit the ideal of being female. They intentionally display stereotypical attributes, thereby remaining recognizable as women, as they go about attending to the demands of the jobs.

Women have to exhibit some degree of femininity to be accepted and some degree of masculinity to be seen as viable in the workplace. It is exhausting and stressful for many women to walk this tightrope. For many women, it is a choice that must be made sometimes daily and sometimes hourly. The choice is often one of being seen as competent (masculine) as is expected of leader or as likeable (feminine) as is expected of women.

In the 2016 presidential election, evidence showed there were as just many anti-Hillary votes as there were pro-Donald votes. Many voters just didn't like her. Again, liking is much more important for women than men. This is largely a product of stricter gender norms and more acute judgement. As was the case in 2016, being disliked can have huge consequences. Much of the fallout from sexism can be based on nothing but personal, hard-to-put-a-reason-to-it bias. While many people could say why they didn't like Hillary, just as many were hard put to do so.

For too many women all of this seems a game that can't be won, a moving target that can't be hit unless a woman is able to be very flexible in turning on and off traits at the right time. This means being gender flexible, gender fluid, or my preference, gender agile, as will be discussed in a later chapter.

Anti-Femininity

It is easily argued that much of gender bias is directed at femininity itself as much as it's directed at women. When it comes to the workplace, many see no place for femininity. Masculinity is seen as the default superior.

In a study I read too many years ago to recall fully, nine-year-olds were asked to write an essay describing how they would feel if they woke up as the other sex. Boys used words like *nightmare* and *horror* and said they "would rather be dead." Girls said more positive things like "more powerful" and "more opportunities." Very early on femininity is stigmatized through socialization.

According to identification theory, seeing women as inferior is an important component of masculinity.

So, it can be said that masculinity has devaluation of femininity built into it. In order to be realized, masculinity is raised in stature and femininity has to be tamped down, diminished, and subjugated. Unfortunately, there are many men who do devalue femininity or otherwise put much space between themselves and femininity as means to bolster their masculinity. And this does happen in the workplace.

These views devalue some very valuable workplace traits and skills. And they devalue women.

While many of the issues women face in the workplace can be traced to patriarchal roots, there is no blame here suggesting that men are the sole practitioners of gender bias, regulation, and devaluation. It may not be so evident, but women, too, prefer some gender lines to be drawn. Some women have double standards and use masculine traits themselves to their own advantage and rebuke other women for doing the same thing. Other women may use or want to use masculine traits, but they admonish men for using feminine ones. And men peer-police each other about masculine rules of behavior, and they do so across a spectrum of severity.

Men as a group are not immune from harm. Though it may not be recognized or considered, men are hampered by sexist expectations also. Research demonstrates that men face backlash when they don't adhere to masculine gender stereotypes—when they show vulnerability, act nicer, display empathy, express sadness, exhibit modesty, and proclaim to be feminists. This is troubling. For one thing, it discourages men from behaving in ways known to benefit their teams and their own careers. And it prevents many men from acquiring new, highly beneficial skills that are seen as more feminine than masculine.

Despite anyone's perception of whether and how much men are saddled with adherence to gender norms, policing does occur. And it starts, as it does with girls, in childhood. In Western society, most boys are strongly admonished against exhibiting any soft traits and taught to shy away from all things feminine.

Men are still expected to follow the man rules and "man up." I have consciously deepened my voice many times to stay on safe ground when I knew there were costs to straying outside the box. The box dictates than men be manly in attitude, appearance, and behavior. The costs of not doing so are many, including jeopardized credibility. Masculine men are given more credibility than men who are less so. In the workplace, this credibility issue affects one's ability as a leader, one's trust as a workmate, and the evaluation of one's work efforts.

This is not to say, however, that male privilege doesn't still hold sway in the workplace.

In male-dominated workplaces, male privilege still allows men to be largely undisturbed by gender concerns in terms of ramifications.

In saying oppositional sexism is a bane to all, I will also point out that another group that greatly suffers from this is LGBTQ+ people, who are, or are perceived to be, outside societal gender norms. And of this group, gay men and trans women may be the most harried to a degree few can imagine. These people, if they even dare share these facets of self, operate in constant awareness of that they are being evaluated, and any perceived gender transgressions are judged most harshly of all.

In closing this chapter, let me say that it was not the intent here to lay out all of the sources of problems—there are many forms of discrimination and burdens that create disparity. For example, misogyny, the extreme of female sexism, or competitiveness between women, whereby women will do intentional personal and professional harm to other women to undermine them within the organization. Rather than identifying all forms of egregious workplace disparities, I hope the point was made clear that imbalance exacerbates disparate and harmful behaviors, and more often does so at greater cost to women than men.

Gender-imbalanced organizations are more problematic.

Chapter 2

Gendered Traits

If the goal is a workplace that is balanced, one where everyone is fully valued and empowered, it should be readily apparent that arbitrary devaluation is a huge hindrance.

Masculine Traits Valued, Feminine Traits Devalued

Devaluation of traits that are considered feminine, traits that affect performance, is a huge workplace concern. Overt bias all too often devalues and obscures a number of valuable feminine traits. For example, being a strong leader (considered masculine) is more valued than being a cooperative leader (considered feminine), and technical skills (considered masculine) are more highly valued than relational skills (considered feminine). Yet, it can be said that 15% of a leader's success is technical ability while a whopping 85% is emotional intelligence (aka EQ, emotional quotient) and people skills. So, the question to be asked is, which sex's skill set do you believe is more valued in more workplaces?

The reality is that in many imbalanced workplaces dominant male traits are the traits that are valued. For example, decisiveness (associated more with men) is given more weight than empathy (associated more with women). Indeed, in practice this becomes "Never mind your emotions, make a sound logical decision." You can guess which behavior will be rewarded and which admonished. Employees, staff, and especially leaders are told to be decisive. That certainly can be a good thing in the right situation. But the high valuation of decisiveness leaves little, if any, practical room for empathy. The two could coexist, but the valuation subjugates one to the other in practice.

Before going further, let's step back and take a higher-level view of gendered traits.

First, let's clear up a bit of this false logic. It goes something like this: more women than men are more feminine than masculine, and tenderness is a feminine trait. Therefore, all women are tender, and as all women are tender, all women are therefore feminine. The same logic is ascribed to men all having specific masculine traits, and all men being masculine. Such logic might not be intentionally afflictive of someone, but it is what perpetuates stereotypes, and stereotypes can be quite harmful. Many people simply choose to believe all women are feminine and all men are masculine. Or they may wish it so, or expect it to be so.

We are wrong in affixing traits to a particular gender.

When we say women are sensitive, for example, such an assignment can be a leap. While there may be some statistical evidence, this perception is based largely on anecdotal or stereotypical shortcuts. Without question, most people accept generalizations and stereotypes as givens. Yet, it is far more accurate to say that being sensitive is a feminine trait that statistically more women exhibit then men. Men can and do have this trait, but it has been socially checked, which limits its frequency, depth, and range. In reality, and depending on a host of factors that we will explore, any one man can be more sensitive than any one woman. Without exploring these things on an individual level, rather than on a generalized level, we are taking shortcuts, the easy route. That likely will not be the route to correct conclusions.

Another big caveat concerning gender trait assignment is that gender traits are often simply miscategorized. More often than not, our behavioral traits are products of something other than gender. For example, traits may be a product of our generation. And many traits are matters of personality. Here's an example: it is often said that men and women lead differently. Rather than being caused by gender, however, a bigger factor may be where a person was born and raised. The *where* is important because leadership style and behaviors can be products of culture. There are huge differences between Eastern and Western leadership, for example. Mathematical ability is another example. The stereotype is that women are not as good at math as men, but internationally, more math competitors (and competition winners) are women. Stereotypes further suggest that Asians are the best at math. This may seem a case where culture produces a trait, but the reality is that it is much more a matter of education. In fact, most traits can be said to be products of some form of education. Formal and social education influences traits more than any other factor.

Leveraging Gender Traits

It is important to understand that differences can be leveraged, with each having its own merit. Here are a couple of examples. Most research attests that women in general are less impulsive. Overall, women take fewer risks than most men. That is neither a bad thing nor necessarily a good thing. It depends on the situation. Research also indicates that men tend to be more unyielding, while women tend to be more flexible. Again, the benefit of either is wholly situational. Leveraging either side of these traits in the right situation can be extremely beneficial.

Having a balance of traits present and leveraging them is a huge organizational plus.

Understanding the concept of gendered traits is prerequisite to understanding how to leverage gender traits for better performance.

In defining gender via traits, we must first categorize the traits themselves as masculine or feminine. Fortunately, this has already been done for us. Society has labeled gender traits. Aggression, for example, is considered a masculine trait. Most see a person with a high propensity for aggression or obvious exhibition of aggressive behaviors as masculine. Conversely, passivity is seen to be feminine. Gender trait determinations are social constructs.

It is never correct to affix traits to either sex exclusively.

It is more accurate to say traits have gender than to say the genders have designated traits.

There are masculine and feminine traits, and it can be said that trait A is a masculine trait and trait B is a feminine one. More importantly, either sex can exhibit either or both traits in varying degrees. For example, rather than saying men are risk-takers, it is more accurate to say that risk-taking is a masculine trait. It is a trait either gender can possess in some measure, even though men may statistically exhibit risky behaviors more often than women.

If we were to use a scale to plot a person's gender makeup, we could say some people are more masculine or feminine than others.

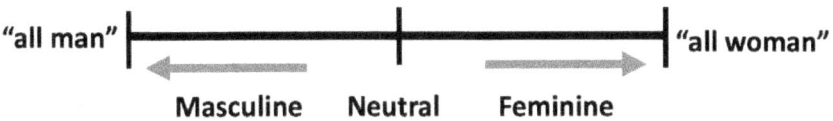

Yet when it comes to a person's makeup, this fails to paint a complete picture for a number of reasons, and it is outright deceptive in other regards.

It is incorrect to label the ends of the spectrum "man" and "woman." Gender is, and should be, kept separate from sex. A person doesn't have to be male to be exceedingly masculine; nor does a person need to be female to be exceedingly feminine. Certainly, some people are overall more masculine than feminine, and some are more feminine than masculine. At the same time, we must acknowledge and be comfortable with the notion that *not all women are feminine, and not all men are masculine.*

Any person may fit anywhere along the scale, and that needs to be accepted by all.

Another big shortcoming of the model is that it is a singular, linear model. It illustrates what many believe: masculinity and femininity are mutually exclusive, exact opposites on a unidimensional model. In the past, even academics erroneously believed that a person who possessed strong masculine traits had weak or few feminine traits, and vice versa. Thus, a person could be plotted as a single point on the masculine-feminine scale. Again, that is incorrect.

Masculinity and femininity are componential.

Women may exhibit multiple individual feminine traits more often than men, and men may exhibit multiple individual masculine traits more often than woman. For example, directness is considered an individual masculine trait, and empathy is considered an individual feminine trait. But anyone can be both direct and empathic to varying degrees.

When a scale model is used, it is better to plot individual masculine and feminine traits rather than assembling masculinity and femininity. Individual gender traits can be put on a separate scale for any one individual, male or female. Take aggression, for example. For any individual, this trait could be plotted alone by placing "completely passive" at one end of the scale and "violently aggressive" at the other. Anything from "neutral" to "violently aggressive" would be considered masculine, and anything from "neutral" to "completely passive" would be considered feminine. All gender traits vary by degree along a spectrum.

Gender Trait Fluidity

This brings us to another flaw with our gender model. It doesn't (obviously) demonstrate fluidity.

Rather than a static plotted point, masculinity and femininity and their compositional traits are fluid.

People move back and forth along the scale by means of their gender behaviors (exhibition of traits). Oftentimes, this movement occurs in very dynamic fashion. This fluidity is actually quite beneficial in workplace performance, and yet fluidity can be restricted for any number of reasons.

Imagine a stereo with digital bars that represent bass, treble, and so on. As music plays, the bars move up and down with the music but not in unison with each other. These bars are like traits. Our multiple and distinct traits are stronger and weaker at various times as they adjust to situations. Such adjustments occur all day of every workday.

Gender traits are not exclusive to one biological sex or the other.

All humans have a mix of gender traits that co-exist.

All men have a varying measure of masculine traits as well as traits more commonly considered feminine, and all women have a varying measure of feminine traits as well as traits more commonly considered masculine. Any individual can have strong masculine traits and weak feminine traits, weak masculine traits and strong feminine traits, or any mixture of both. Again, any person can be concurrently decisive, which is considered a masculine trait, and empathetic, which is considered a feminine trait. (It seems all of us have been lied to by at least one nursery rhyme author. Snails indeed. Hmph!)

The components themselves should be plotted as a compilation in

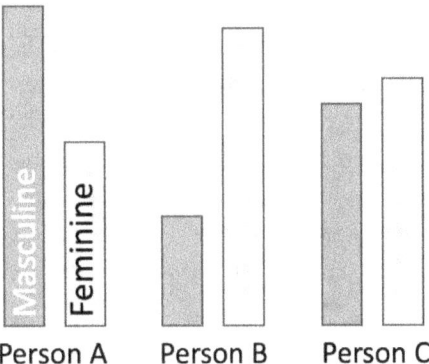

a nonsingular manner. Plotting gender could be done on a two-dimensional model with a scale for masculinity that plots high to low and a second scale for femininity that tracks high to low. A person's gender can be plotted on both scales simultaneously in a nonexclusive manner with each bar representing a compilation of the person's masculine and feminine traits. Even here, however, the fluid nature of gender and gender traits is not well represented.

This model varies considerably from the spectrum model shown earlier. With this model, more masculine does not mean less feminine, and more feminine does not mean less masculine.

I have been told I can be disconnected (aloof), and yet I have been also told that I'm a great listener (feminine trait). These traits are not mutually exclusive; rather, they exist side by side. I have many such gender traits, as we all do.

All of this may seem obvious, but a number of people cling tightly to gender dichotomy. When it comes to anything relating to gender, many people want black-and-white difference—the singular spectrum where men and women are opposites. The fact is, however, that studies show men and women have more traits in common than not.

When it comes to people (workers, staff, and leaders), there are not risk-takers and non-risk-takers, but there are people who operate with varying degrees of risk and caution. Again, these traits are more fluid than static.

Gender traits are also relative. For example, risky decisions only seem risky when they are compared to cautious logic or to the environment in which risky or cautious decisions are made. Decisions by a person who generally exhibits a high degree of logic may seem risky only as a matter of behaving uncharacteristically in a given situation. Decisions made in a workplace where high risk is a norm may seem not so risky at all. Compared to caution, in general, the perception of risk is heightened.

Gender traits are also situational. Who we are with, where we are, and what is at hand at any given point determines traits we exhibit. For example, while competitiveness may be accepted as more typically a male trait, women may be much more so in given situations. People also behave differently—generally more in line with gender stereotypes—in homogeneous groups. A man, for example, may be more aggressive or risky with other men but more reserved and/or empathetic with women. The environment itself has been shown to affect traits. Men and women will adjust behavior to fit the perceived nature of the environment. If an environment *looks* like a men's locker room, for example, women will exhibit masculine traits more than they might otherwise. What traits we adjust in a given situation can vary, and the degree to which we adjust them can be quite substantial. In this we see the fluid nature of traits in play. The ability to adjust and use gender traits can be of great benefit in the workplace. That same fluidity and adjustability can be tools of balance.

Traits can be appropriate or inappropriate to any situation, including workplace situations. For example, women are better observers. They are more aware of things happening around them, especially things that relate to people. The feminine trait of awareness is a good thing in dynamic complex situations and/or situations with many moving pieces. Awareness can be a bad trait when it is used in the wrong situation. For example, a penchant to be highly aware could actually be a distraction in a situation where focus and concentration are needed. Leveraging either side of any trait by both men and women in the right situation can be very beneficial. The problem is that imbalanced organizations simply do not have a full suite of traits, a full complement of tools, to apply appropriately to all situations.

As much as gender traits vary in different situations, they similarly vary with motivation.

For example, it is widely accepted that women are better at discerning emotion. The reality is that women do *not* have greater empathetic ability. Rather, they are motivated to use empathy skills more often than men. Sometimes what serves as motivation are subtle (usually societal) cues that can remind a woman to be empathetic. For example, parents often advise girls to be more understanding in situations such as fighting with friends. Thus, there is parental motivation to be empathetic. Women typically do better with empathy because it is more emotionally important to them in being part of social circles, which is something they are taught as a priority for girls.

Various studies found that most (up to 98%) of humans have empathy hardwired in their brains. Women, however, still tend to be more empathic in general largely due to social conditioning. Yet men score nearly equally with women in empathetic ability when the studies have included a motivation factor. When men are motivated, they can be as empathetic as women if the situation is one in which sensitivity is socially acceptable for men. More typically, however, men are encouraged to operate more from logic than from emotion. Thus, while most men have strong empathetic abilities, they don't often exercise them because of lack of motivation.

Motivation can result from subtle or overt messaging such as "men should" or "women should." For example, tell a woman she is good at consensus-building or tell a man he is a strong, directive leader, and they both try to do all they can to live up to the expectation.

The situational and motivational nature of gender traits is extremely important because it attests to flexible use of appropriate skills that may benefit an organization.

Motivation is especially worth attention because it is highly controllable in the workplace. Consider, for example, what motivations might be present in a male-dominated workplace or a female-dominated workplace.

Ultimately, an organization should strive for a mix of traits among its people. This might suggest the solution is numerical—an equal mix of men and women. But recall that while a trait may be common to one sex or the other, it is not inextricably bound to one sex or other. That again supports that balance in numbers of men and women in an organization matters less than balance in contribution and influence wrought by utilization. What we want to focus on is using masculine and feminine traits in the workplace to achieve balance and reap the greatest amount of performance. The fluidity and malleability of gendered traits are the real keys to balance.

But before we get there, we need to note and clarify a few additional caveats about traits and further heighten understanding of their plasticity.

We often see traits as binary and not as fluid on a varying scale.

Stereotypes, including gender stereotypes, cause us to overestimate differences between groups and underestimate variability within groups.

We see large differences between groups where little if any exists to begin with. Furthermore, traits themselves can be misunderstood or misinterpreted. For example, a tentative communication style does not mean a speaker actually feels tentative or lacks confidence, though it may be interpreted so. Similarly, many people are unable to discern between confidence and competence. Confidence is often confused for competence. And we often lose sight of the lesser traits in a person when we see only the greater. For example, both sexes are competitive, but the masculine form is far more overt. So even while a great many women are also competitive, that is lost among the overtly competitive men. People also lose sight of subtlety. Finally, we need to remember that categorizing traits as masculine and feminine is social construct and, thus, subject to change.

Sources of Gender Traits

Next, we will look at sources of gender traits. The intent is not to dissect fully where gender traits are derived from but rather to illuminate ways traits can be acquired or cross-utilized.

There is an ongoing debate about the cause of traits being nature or nurture—socialization versus biology.

Overwhelmingly, scholars and professionals agree that most masculine and feminine traits and behaviors are products of social constructs.

For example, the perceived female trait of being passive is more accurately non-expression of aggression and is thus largely due to social constraint. Society typically hasn't allowed women as many opportunities as men to practice aggressive behaviors. This, of course, is socialization. The same takes place when young girls are rewarded for being modest and deferring, and boys are rewarded for being bold and commanding.

Conditioning for alignment with gender norms begins in childhood. Children come to understand their gender as they mature by watching and learning from other men and women, especially adults. A child learns early that women are expected to be pleasant nurturing, and men are to be assertive, ambitious, dominant, and self-centered.[22]

In play, boys and girls seek out activities through which they can experiment with gendered characteristics. Once a child develops an understanding of their ascribed gender, they strive to behave in norms deemed consistent with that gender.[23]

In childhood play groups, the rules for boys are quite different from the rules for girls. From a very young age, boys taunt each other in mimicking behavior of older boys and men. Boys rehearse taking criticism and, thus, become more thick-skinned or insensitive. In doing so, they instinctively train each other to become self-protective and also to fill the social role of protector. Boy groups are ruled by competition, physical strength, athleticism, and strength of will. Boys practice fighting as the way to the top of the pecking order. Thus, men practice competition and aggression from childhood and throughout their lives. Any boy or man who doesn't exhibit such masculine strengths and who possesses more feminine traits, or appears more feminine, is marginalized. Among girls, there is more negotiation for social positioning, and social skills rule. They learn to cooperate, collaborate and defer. Relational skills such as communications and listening are highly encouraged. Throughout their lives, girls and women receive positive reinforcement of these feminine behaviors. "You two should work it out." "Oh, that was so sweet of you." Boys and men receive positive reinforcement for masculine behaviors. "Stand up for yourself." "Way to be tough, son." Both receive negative reinforcement for "non-gender-appropriate" behaviors. Rules are additionally affected by factors such as generational or cultural differences. The ways men and women are socialized (gendered), and to what extent, also evolve. The rules are being flexed more in more recent times.

All of this says one thing: *traits are not innate to gender but are assigned to individual people.*

When we say women exhibit trait A and men exhibit trait B, we are really saying that statistically women are more inclined to exhibit trait A than men. When we say men are better at this task or women are better at that task, we must also take into account that men are better versed in this one and women are more practiced in the other. When we say women are more sensitive, for example, it is because women as a group, more so than men as a group, have an emotional range that has been given more practice. The socially acceptable range of emotions and personable behaviors is more limited for men and, thus, far less exercised.

We cannot dismiss biology altogether, because there is reliable evidence for certain gender trait assignments via biology. One example pertains to Asperger syndrome. Awareness is a feminine trait; focus is a masculine trait. Intense focus (a trait) can be a symptom of Asperger syndrome, as can disconnectedness and unawareness. The scientific community has concluded Asperger syndrome is directly related to amounts of testosterone, a hormone. Asperger syndrome disorder in men has a proven biological cause and can be used as evidence of biological causation of traits. Likewise, other biological influences, such as hormones, brain structure, and so on, might contribute to other gender traits.

What is most relevant here? Most traits are products of socialization and are learned over time. In 1987 Candace West and Don Zimmerman introduced the idea that gender is something one does as opposed to who one is.[24] People act, or "do" *male* or *female* based on roles or characteristics learned through social interaction.

In the end, traits are for the most part something that a person is better versed in or practiced at as a result of social influencing. Any trait can be exhibited by either sex, and more important for our purposes, any trait can be acquired by either sex.

Traits are adoptable and adaptable, and each of us is ductile.

In this way, one's gender can, in a sense, be described as fluid. You possess the ability to move along the gender scale and do so with individual traits—your characteristics and behaviors. Traits are realized as behaviors that vary in degree and expression at different times and in different places.

Gender Traits in the Workplace

The behaviors of interest here are those that represent workplace skills. Again, take empathy (a feminine trait), for example. Empathy is finally getting due recognition as a workplace asset. Many organizations now recognize and leverage empathy as an acceptable workplace behavior and also encourage it more. Organizations recognize its value to both performance and service. In fact, many organizations are trying to instill empathy as part of workplace culture. Empathy is a skill—a skill both sexes have but one that is more limited and less honed in men because they have not practiced it as women have.

The traits that determine success in the office, on the field, in the classroom, on the factory floor, and in every aspect of life are not exclusive to one gender or another. We are all malleable.

The upper hand is held by individuals most able and willing to be fluid with masculine and feminine traits, regardless of their sex at birth.

Studies have shown that high school boys who were perceived as more feminine and high school girls who were perceived as more masculine scored higher on the National Merit Scholarship qualifying tests than male peers firmly at the masculine end of the masculine/feminine spectrum and women peers more fixed at the feminine end of the scale. Why? Fluid individuals have the ability to better acquire cross-gender skills, which gives them a fuller set of skills from which to draw. Successful leaders are able to be both intellectual and emotional, exhibiting both masculine and feminine traits. *Gender fluidity increases performance.* And organizations benefit when employees are encouraged to be fluid in the use of gender traits.

Any leader worth their salt knows that individual success and organizational success are inextricably linked. People up and down the line in an organization need to leverage their full suite of traits and acquire new ones to the same end, and they need to encourage others to do the same.

Let's look at one example of different masculine and feminine traits being utilized in the workplace: interviewing techniques. A masculine interviewing style (detached) would be more prevalent in an androcentric environment, and a feminine interviewing style (relational) would be more prevalent in a gynocentric environment. It can be surmised that using both interviewing methodologies would yield the most data and better conclusions.

An analogy can be drawn comparing varied approaches in a lab or office or on a retail floor to a sports field. Team sports require a variety of skills—a mix of skilled players adept at the talents needed for their positions. These sports skills could be called offensive and defensive skills. In the workplace, we'd say masculine and feminine skills. Most teams succeed with a balance. Furthermore, any player coached appropriately could wield either skill set.

Balance, however, does not always happen. Certainly, a part of the reason is simply an imbalance in numbers.

The core issue of imbalance, however, is really a matter of power, how much one sex's traits and skills are valued, and how much one sex is permitted to use its traits and skills to contribute and influence.

Returning to a sports analogy, the proficient rebounder needs to be as valued as the proficient three-point shooter, and a Golden Glove winner as valued as an RBI champion.

Expectations, Pushback, and Reluctance

As a relatively recent change in the Western workplace, women are encouraged to "lean in," be strong, stand up and take charge, or even "lead like a man." In encouraging women in this, there is at least an element of a double standard. In some places and situations, women are freer to express masculinity in various forms, and women have more outlets for exhibiting masculine traits. But men are scorned for nearly all expressions of femininity. For example:

- **Showing vulnerability.** Men are socialized to not ask for help or be vulnerable—and they can be penalized when they challenge this notion. An informative set of studies from 2015 finds that when male (but not female) leaders ask for help, they are viewed as less competent, capable, and confident.[25] And when men make themselves vulnerable by disclosing a weakness at work, they are perceived to have lower status. This is problematic, as not seeking help when you need it or admitting areas for improvement inevitably leads to mistakes and less development.

- **Being nicer.** Given that many of us want more nice guys at work, we might assume that men would be celebrated for being calm and unassuming. Wrong. Research has found that men who are more communal and agreeable (e.g., warm, caring, supportive, sympathetic) made significantly less money than more stereotypically masculine men. More agreeable men across multiple industries made an average of 18% less in income and were evaluated as less likely to have management potential as compared to less agreeable men. Similarly, "nice guys" were evaluated as less competent and less hirable for managerial roles. One experimental study found that male managers in consulting who tended to advocate more for their team than for themselves were judged to be lower in agency and competence and more likely to be considered for job dismissal.[26] Unfortunately, given the costs—real and psychological—of being a nice guy at work, men may be less likely to engage in these behaviors, which could help their own career and make them better colleagues.

- **Displaying empathy.** Empathy is an important part of leadership. However, women are more likely to receive "credit" for it than men. A recent study found that female leaders who displayed empathy (as reported by their employees) were less likely to be in danger of career derailment—e.g., problems with interpersonal relationships, difficulty building and leading teams, difficulty changing and adapting, failure in meeting business goals and objectives, and having too narrow a functional orientation. Men did not get this boost—there was no relationship between male leaders' empathy and their bosses' assessment of potential career derailment. These findings are consequential because displaying empathy is critical for leading effectively.

As has been said repeatedly now, where personal masculine or feminine traits are, in a sense, prohibited it is not only a personal issue but also a matter of organizational performance. Consider, for example, that research has shown successful teams have three things in common. First, successful teams have more than an average number of women—that, of course, being a matter of numbered balance. Second, members of successful teams all contributed equally—this being contribution parity, as I call it. And third, successful teams have social sensitivity. Ugh, that word *sensitivity*! There are those who would pause or balk right here. The use of the word alone—*sensitivity*—will turn some away from these best practices even knowing a more successful team could be result.

When was the last time you heard anything positive said about being sensitive in the workplace? Yet, sensitivity can be very valuable in the right situation, including workplace situations. Feminine traits are a necessity in today's workplace. This as evidenced by any number of studies. And yet these necessary traits are seen as *less than* masculine traits. Feminine traits are seen as weaker. Traits associated with masculinity (such as assertiveness and resourcefulness) have positive connotations, while showing emotion (primarily a feminine trait) is considered irrational. Social behaviors that actually enhance influence for women, the very thing we need for balance, are seen often as nonwork, a waste of time, or even social manipulation.

As much as some industries are now recognizing the value of feminine skills, this is still far from universal. It certainly can't yet be said that it is common even in Western society. There is still a devaluation of feminine skills in most workplaces. As testament to that devaluation, let me start with the fact that feminine skills are still referred to as *soft skills*.

Not only are soft skills themselves devalued, but the terminology associated with them has itself become a joke.

The term *soft skills* is often snickered at in many circles. Consider how many times you have heard the term used as a pejorative or how often you see people using air quotes when they say it. This is nothing short of derision aimed not only at the words but also at what they represent.

While training in both masculine skills and feminine skills is very valuable, it's a hard sell to men, the very people who would benefit the most. In a great many webinars that I have conducted on soft skills, attendance by women has far outpaced attendance by men.

Reluctance of men to gain cross-gender skills is often a matter of lifelong conditioning and stigmatizing femininity in boys, and it is difficult to overcome. In one series of experiments, college students were paid to be photographed. They had a choice of one or another gender-typical tasks, such as nailing boards together or ironing cloth napkins. Most chose the one most closely related to their own gender, even though the pay was substantially higher for the other.

In the workplace, just ask some male workers or leaders to attend "feminine-skills training" or even "gender training," and see how many will run for the exit doors. Getting men into such training can actually require disguising the training title.

I started this chapter by suggesting that devaluation of all things feminine is nothing short of villainy. This villain's victims are both male and female. For women, what they have to offer in the workplace is too often devalued. For men, their success, recognized or not, in many cases falls short of their potential.

Chapter 3

Imbalance

One study shows that women perform better in warmer temperatures.[27] In the study, 543 students in Berlin were asked to do match calculations without a calculator, write as many words as possible given a string of random letters, and answer questions in a cognitive reflection test. In two out of three of these exercises (math and verbal), women performed much better at higher room temperatures and men performed better at lower room temperatures. The gender performance effect of temperature change was very strong and directly impacted productivity.

The performance information in this may be new to you, but I don't think it comes as any surprise that men and women have different preferences when it comes to the thermostat. Nor do I believe it comes as surprise to most people that it is men who win the thermostat wars in most workplaces. You could say that the ambient environment in most workplaces is androcentric, and as such it is not only uncomfortable for women, but it is also a disadvantage.

We are not here to talk androcentric and gynocentric in terms of temperature, however. Rather we want to frame it in terms of work culture.

Organizational culture may lean male or female. And each culture has a set of preferred and often enforced behaviors, views, values, methodologies, and so on. Leaning male (male-centric/androcentric) or leaning female (female-centric/gynocentric) is by definition imbalance.

Androcentric vs. Gynocentric

The majority of companies, organizations, and institutions are still androcentric.

In fact, in a recent LinkedIn post a friend and colleague of mine, Julie Kratz of Pivot Point (nextpivotpoint.com), challenged readers to name an industry that is female dominated. And she went on to write that "the usual answers are: non-profit, health care, and education. While women are employed at higher levels in these industries, they are not equally represented at a leadership level. While women make up 76% of teachers in the US, they are only 16% of university presidents and 52% of principals. Women are 70% of the health care industry's workers, and just 30% of leadership team members. In non-profit, women are just 18% of CEO's while they are 75% of the workforce."

This is not to say there cannot be any female-dominated cultures. Numbers alone can, and at times do, influence culture. But gynocentric cultures are very much a rarity. Furthermore, organizations may stay culturally androcentric even when the numbers are more balanced. Androcentric cultures can be hyper-masculine, or less so. While not all male-dominated environments have the outward appearance of such, the culture is still there.

In a male-dominated culture, doing things the male way is still the accepted way to operate, to relate to others, to be rewarded, and to get ahead.

For example, there is the perception that an extended workday equals success. An extended workday may be a cultural expectation, a requirement, of the job. However, while it might be expected, it should also be seen as gender-insensitive, given the family demands largely still placed on women. And even where such gender insensitivity is recognized, many write it off as not an organizational issue but more one of personal choice. In not challenging such cultural practices and accepting a "that's just the way it is" attitude, lopsidedness persists.

Androcentric Conformance vs. Feminine Preference

As more workplaces are androcentric, women are faced with two choices: adapt and assimilate into the male-dominated environment in order to participate, or withdraw.

More often it is the former.

How much conformance is necessitated may vary, with some organizations or institutions being more or less rigid in this regard. The gender makeup of an organization does affect this. In many places, if you are in the majority you get more leeway in exercising traits, styles, methodologies, and so on. On the other hand, there are some places where majority privilege doesn't hold sway, but rather the institution itself allows or restricts more freedoms for all. The arts and humanities can be a place of lessened rigidity, for example. But there are also environments where the rules are lax on one side of the coin but not the other. For example, a female police officer would have freedom to be more aggressive, but that does not mean the masculine rules for men will be lessened in the same environment. These are just a few examples of institutional exception. Other factors can greatly influence the acceptance and enforcement of gender rules, race being one.

In many organizations women have to adapt to many facets of their androcentric environments. For example, most androcentric environments are extremely insular and/or competitive. There tends to be a reverence for individual achievement and individualism more aligned with masculine preferences. Androcentric environments often lack opportunities for cooperation and collaboration, which are modes favored by more women. From the time women are little girls, they are taught to take turns and to defer to others. Thus, women are more socialized to be, and more socially expected to be, "team players." Women also typically bond through the support of others as a product of their socialization and thus prefer not to be isolated. Deference to masculine individualism, authority, and "top dog" thinking butts heads with feminine collaboration.

Male-centric, male-favored cultures often lack rewards for collaboration. Rather, rewards are based on competitive wins. It's not that women can't compete and succeed in such arenas or are not interested in doing so, but studies show that competing causes discomfort and stress for many women. It is a performance issue because competition can cause a lessening of female performance. In one English study, women ran faster times when running by themselves against a clock than against others. Women will also negotiate harder for others (a collaborative behavior) than they will for themselves (seen as competitive). As for men, competing boosts male performance. Many men actually get bio-physical rewards from competition, and they eagerly embrace a winner-take-all mentality. Of course, there are exceptions among either sex.

I often use a word in my instruction to describe a male phenomenon: *cooper-tition*. Cooper-tition is how many men view how they work *with* others. In "competition with" others is seen as "work with" others. It is how they see top performance realized by all as a group. While sales is an obvious example, I will use another sports analogy. Cooper-tition could be likened to a track team in which members of the team race against others, including members or their own team. Despite individual competition, what is being achieved is a team score as the result of individual placement—a team score that goes against other teams (organizations). Those that embrace the concept of cooper-tition cheer each other on in their own way and congratulate each other for their wins. This is a positive and not a negative way of doing business for many men.

This is not to say that any number of women can't or don't embrace competition or cooper-tition. No doubt thousands of examples to the contrary could be cited. But many women see any form of competition as just that—competition with winners and losers, not the way most women would prefer to operate.

The effects of being cemented male-centric are not just personal. A lack of team collaboration hurts organizations also. Excessive competition can also cause a lack of female participation and contribution altogether. Organizations would much benefit from being more balanced in competitive and collaborative approaches.

Androcentric and Gynocentric Work Processes

Work can be androcentric or gynocentric in a number of ways. Differences can include methodologies, organization of work, relational behaviors, and so on. In the realm of research, for example, the masculine approach tends to be more concrete, looking at the depersonalized, dissected, definitive parts piecemeal or mechanically. In contrast, an approach that is more contextual, looks more at cause and effect, and tends to choose larger cross sections and relationships between components is more feminine. Men are typically more interested in definitive properties (detached dissection), while women prefer to listen to characteristics and how they are associated with systems around them (more intuitive observation). Men favor impersonal observation (e.g., they study brains in terms of chemicals, brain wave patterns), while women's studies tend to be more hands-on (e.g., Jane Goodall's groundbreaking work with primates).

Another example of gender differences in approaches is interviewing technique. Interviewing could be seen as a feminine approach to gathering information. After all, it's personal interaction. However, interviewing is quite often a masculine approach to data gathering, which favors men. Men prefer to be detached in getting to the root, and interviews can be conducted that way. But let's also consider that interviewing is often done in a situation of power imbalance, where the interviewer is in a position of authority to ask questions, and the interviewee is obligated on some level to defer to the authority and answer the questions posed to them. The right to ask a person a question and expect an answer is a point of power. Because men are historically given more authority than women, it is often easier for men to be interviewers. Thus, it is a male-advantaged approach.

Of course, a detached, authoritarian approach is not the only way to conduct interviews. Interviewing can be more interpersonal and connective. The goal of interviewing can also be more feminine in looking less for concrete data points and more for connections. Women can be successful interviewers from a more relational approach, an approach that may put the interviewee in a more eased emotional state that allows information to flow more freely. There are pros and cons to each interviewing approach.

The point is, of course, that using various interviewing styles yields more types of data. This is far more likely to occur in a balanced organization. In an imbalanced organization, not only would data be limited, per our example, but one gender has to defer to the other in technique or risk consequences of not doing it the majority way (the accepted "right" way).

Communication is another area of general gender difference. In practice, communications can be androcentric or gynocentric. Successful organizations freely use a myriad of communications modes, mediums, approaches, and styles. While many organizations recognize the value in this, some recognize it only in part. Many organizations have very broad and strategic public communications practices, ones that accommodate both male and female preferences. Yet a number of these same organizations give little thought to internal communication practices. Internally, the majority of institutions still favor direct and assertive (masculine) communication styles.

Face-to-face communications actually favor men. As in the interviewing example, men more often than women are given automatic authority. And men, perhaps simply as a result of that automatic authority, are more confident in their communications. Women tend to be quieter overall, especially in mixed groups. They are less likely to ask questions or make their opinions known, and they seldom initiate dialog, even in office settings, when men are present. Studies find that women speak less overall in male-dominated or mixed groups. And when they do speak, women are interrupted more often than men by both men and women.

In many organizations, visibility is another process that is hugely important to personal success, and this too favors men. Far too often, women defer and let men get the attention. This is much more prevalent in male-dominated cultures and environments. Women turn down speaking events twice as often as men do, for example. Even when women are eager to participate, there are far fewer opportunities for women to publish or speak. When voice and visibility are denied, so too is influence. Organizations lose out when women's voices are missing or the volume thereof is too low.

Obviously, any pursuit benefits from the use of all types of approaches. To do so, however, requires an organization to be balanced. A lack of balance causes fewer approaches and leads to fewer possibilities for outcomes and, thus, limited success options.

(Female) Assimilation vs. Authenticity

A large part of the problem is historical roots. In many professions, women were *allowed* in rather than accepted as worthy. That's especially true in institutionalized professions. In fact, the origins of some professions were entirely set up to exclude women. Integration was an act of assimilation while leaving the institution undisturbed and unchanged. Success was largely a matter of conformity, at least until critical mass was reached. For the record, critical mass in anything is reached at about 15%. Before that, the environment is all conformance. Once critical mass is reached, the environment very slowly begins to move away from status quo and conformance.

On the surface this may seem purely a numbers issue. But there is more below the surface. Organizations that value conformity at the expense of authenticity incur hidden costs.

People who are allowed to be authentic bring their whole selves to their jobs and participate fully and openly in the workplace. They add more to the benefit of the organization and the people it serves. In environments of stubborn conformance, unique skills and knowledge go unutilized, traits are devalued, and contributions are tamped down.

Women especially must balance authenticity and subversion.

To *fit* in many professions women often shed valuable attributes that seem to be liabilities.

Women often jettison some aspects of femininity, no small number of which are feminine traits that are quite valuable in the workplace. Women will "dumb down" and do other self-deprecating things to conform to the male-centric environment and to gender stereotypes. And they pick up masculine traits in an effort to conform to the perceived requirements of the culture and be "one of the guys."

The energy expended trying to come across as something one is not is energy unavailable for work and other activities.

A good female friend of mine once told me this: "I adopted more male traits in order to try to fit in at work and at the university, where I chose a male-dominated field. Part of why I chose a male-dominated field was because it paid more money than traditional female jobs. That was not to my advantage, though, career-wise. I adopted traits such as being less talkative, which made it easier to work with male peers, but also came off as standoffish and hence was perceived as unfriendly." I have no doubt whatsoever that while the specifics on how one adapts and the consequences thereof may differ, my friend's story of costly conformance is a common one.

In conforming to androcentric cultures that favor a masculine skill set, women face another problem: women who express more traits more typically associated with men (e.g., aggressive behaviors) are judged harshly.

The necessity for women to conform in a great many workplaces causes women to experience pushback, disempowerment, and relationship problems with both male and female co-workers.

Compounding the issue is that at the same time women are trying to utilize the favored masculine traits in balance with societal expectations, they also being told very loudly to "lean in," "be authentic," "own it," and whatever else the current bestseller says. All this leaves women questioning the right path forward. And the never-ending balance game continues.

Men, on the other hand, don't ask themselves, or need to ask themselves, "Who will I be at work today?" Or "How shall I behave?" Or "What traits and roles will I balance in what fashion?"

There may be some situations or places where men have to make some adjustments, but they are few and far between.

While men can go through their days generally devoid of concerns about their gender, women have to be more conscious of and vigilant about their behaviors. Every day, hour, and minute, women are considering such questions, looking for the right answers, and attempting to adjust their behaviors accordingly.

Insiders, Outsiders, and Disparity

Often women fall short in their effort to adjust appropriately, and they find themselves on the outside looking in. All organizations have *insiders* and *outsiders*. And while there can be a number of factors that put one in the "in group" or in the "out group," gender in an imbalanced workplace is a biggie. At its worst, a gender imbalance skewed male can be fertile soil for the proverbial "good old boys' club."

In too many places the good old boys' club exists as a place of exclusionary power and influence. The good old boys club can also be self-contained cliques in which men hang out with other men exclusive of women. This often occurs when men work and conduct business informally, providing men further value unto themselves while denying organizational and informational assets to women.

Outsiders are denied many things. Some are more tangible, such as funding or even speaking opportunities; others more subtle such as access to people or information.

Imagine the workplace is an unfamiliar city. Men and women are both handed maps to the city, but the map the man gets from other knowledgeable men includes all the street names, points of interest, and the legend. The map the women get handed has a minimum level of labeling. Men thus have all the information necessary to easily navigate; women have to sort more things out for themselves.

In a male-dominated workplace, women are also 20% less likely than men to get needed feedback from their supervisors and 24% less likely than men to get advice from senior leaders.[28] It doesn't take much brainpower to see what a disadvantage that can be for women. Getting 20% less feedback would be like getting a map to an unfamiliar city with 20% of the roads missing.

Where the numbers are lopsided, so too is the power. This lopsidedness causes devaluation of one's work and authority. It can lead to both subtle and outright discrimination. Power is ultimately what our definition of balance is all about—influence and parity therein.

A component of power is legitimacy.

When the power structure is heavily concentrated in one gender, it is harder for the others to be perceived as strong or even perceive themselves as so.

The power group seems legitimate and the non-power group less so. Women may often feel disempowered (unable to contribute and have effect) and may thus act so. Women working in a mixed group get less credit for their work. In technical environments, female leaders are perceived as less technically competent than men. Men are twice as likely to be selected to perform a mathematical calculation on the basis of their gender alone. In the research field and in academia, far too often a woman's paper is questioned as being plagiarized. Similar examples can be found in the legal arena, among sales forces, and so on. In a great many places feminine traits are devalued and are seen as *less than* (or weaker than) masculine traits.

I see it as fittingly descriptive that women are swimming against the current. Swimming against the current is a good analogy because the current is the majority—the majority way of doing things, and the majority having the power. The current in the stream may not look so swift on the surface, but it is quite strong underneath.

Microinequities

Oftentimes the disempowerment is subtle—an undercurrent. For example, women far more than men have their titles dropped when being introduced—"This is Anne" rather than "This is Dr. Brown." This is an example of a microinequity or microaggression.

Microinequities are cumulative, subtle messages that promote negative bias and demoralize. They tend to be directed at members of underrepresented groups in an organization. Examples include:

- Checking emails or texting during a face-to-face conversation.
- Consistently mispronouncing a person's name.
- Interrupting a person midsentence.
- Making eye contact only with men while talking to a group of both men and women.
- Taking more questions from men than from women.
- Confusing a person of a certain ethnicity with another person of the same ethnicity.
- Rolling the eyes.
- Mentioning the achievements of some people at a meeting but not others whose achievements are equally relevant.

My colleague Amy C. Waninger explains microaggressions this way:

> These behaviors, called *microaggressions,* are like emotional papercuts that we inflict upon one another, often without realizing it. We say things or make assumptions that are rooted in ignorance or obliviousness, if not outright hostility. But these seemingly small indignities have a big impact over time.[29]

I agree that they are extremely annoying, as well as harmful. Those harms can linger as scars that we are ever aware of. However, I see microaggressions as even more serious—they can be debilitating.

What these seemingly innocuous actions do is disempower.

They take away power and value from those to whom they are directed—generally, minorities. In imbalanced workplaces, not only are such microinequities allowed to exist, they often exist as a matter of culture.

It is in an employer's best interest to snuff out this behavior in order to create a more productive organization. Employees who are treated fairly will ultimately be more engaged and productive in the workplace, whereas employees who experience consistent and continued microaggressive behaviors may find that their very health is impacted. Research findings indicate that microaggressions can lead to increased levels of depression.

Some microinequities affect women uniquely. Women are talked over and interrupted in meetings more than men by both men and women. Oftentimes women are simply ignored in meetings even when they're talking. Mansplaining is a unique type of interruption used by men to exert a dominance perspective, usually over women. Mansplaining is when a man explains something to a woman in a condescending way, assuming she has no knowledge of the subject. This can happen even when the female perspective may be authoritative. Likewise, manterrupting happens when a man interrupts a woman especially excessively.

A study conducted by Northwestern Law School found that Supreme Court Justice Ruth Bader Ginsburg is interrupted six times as often as her male colleagues; Justice Sonia Sotomayor, three times more often; and Justice Elena Kagan, twice as often.[30]

It is worth pointing out that the study also concluded that "women on the Supreme Court…are interrupted at a markedly higher rate" by "both male justices and male advocates."

One very public example of this occurred during the 2009 MTV Video Music Awards, when Kanye West grabbed the mic from Taylor Swift, who had just won an award and was trying her best to accept it. West said, "Imma let you finish, but Beyoncé had one of the best videos of all time." Manterrupting was also evident during the September 2016 presidential debate, when Donald Trump interrupted Hillary Clinton 22 times in the first 26 minutes. Or when Senate Majority Leader Mitch McConnell interrupted Elizabeth Warren's recitation of Coretta Scott King's 1986 letter against Jeff Sessions but allowed Bernie Sanders to read it the next day.

All forms of illegitimating and devaluing leave employees feeling angered, underappreciated, and a thousand other personal emotions. They create permanent personal scars with organizational consequences.

Ramifications, Personal and Organizational

Lest you now assume these issues are black and white, with male insiders besetting upon female outsiders, let me add some gray. In male-dominated organizations, women often turn on other women. The more unbalanced the workplace, the more women bully each other.

An environment of insiders and outsiders is one of discrimination. The more imbalanced an organization, the more forms of discrimination exist for outsiders, and the more severe they are.

Neither androcentric nor gynocentric is a good thing. A male-dominated workplace can be very uncomfortable for many women, and a female-dominated workplace can be very uncomfortable for many men. In general, men and women prefer working with their own sex. A large gender imbalance means that members of one gender or another may naturally feel they're outsiders. There is also evidence that the very environment hurts performance. If an environment looks like a men's locker room or a women's salon, one gender or the other may likewise feel out of place.

At it's worst, when one sex dominates a culture, the other removes themselves.

In her dissertation, Megan Foley noted this:

> For some women, however, changing career tracks was necessary because the masculine culture associated with some alternate career choices was too severe an adjustment to make. This statement came from a cadet who was compelled to change from her original choice to become a pilot: "I used to want to be a fighter pilot, but now I am going into intelligence. The fighter pilots, hanging out every Friday night and going to bars and singing songs that are very demeaning to women…they are able to do that and continue the tradition because there aren't very many women in the field."[31]

As stated previously, androcentric culture necessitates that women and men do things the guy way, and gynocentric the opposite, or otherwise remove themselves. If one chooses to stay, there is the personal effect of having to do things in ways that do no not align well with who they are. I often tell my classes that empowerment and control are mutually exclusive (they are). And likewise, excelling and assimilation are also mutually exclusive. Motivation, interest, and creativity are tamped down in any individual who has to assimilate.

An imbalanced situation can be uncomfortable, stressful, and mentally demanding. Discomfort in any form affects behaviors that, in turn, can hamper success. The fact is that the majority will outperform the minority. Or, more correctly, the empowered will always outperform the undervalued.

A better workplace is one in which members of both sexes feel at home, or at least feel comfortable enough to fully engage and invest in the tasking at hand, rather than feeling distracted or ill at ease.

The personal impacts of being a minority in an imbalanced environment are indeed egregious. I'll wrap up this chapter, however, by getting back to the organizational harms.

Much of my work has been with organizations that had such imbalanced male-female staffing ratios as to hamper the organization. I have witnessed imbalance as a hidden organizational cost. Imagine a business using 1990s software, oblivious to more current technologies. Such a company may operate happily under the belief that they are using technology adequate to meet customer needs and be successful. The truth of the matter, however, is that they are at a serious competitive disadvantage that could not be self-sustaining. Or imbalance could be like a hidden, unrealized weight a racer might carry. A weight that he or she may be used to but that leaves the obliviously hampered racer befuddled at being passed up by so many other lean runners. In reality, a lot of organizational leaders are oblivious to the disadvantages of gender imbalance. These leaders don't see it as the weight it is—a hidden cost to their business and service.

Organizational harms include (but are not limited to):

- **Nonresponsive customer service.** Consider that roughly half of the population is female and the other half male. And then entertain the argument that the needs of male customers, male clients, and male stakeholders may be better understood by male employees and male leaders. Likewise, consider that the needs of female customers, female clients, and female stakeholders may be better understood by female employees and leaders. Full disclosure—I don't believe that is always the case, but I acknowledge there are times when it is. In accepting the original premise, however, it could appropriately be concluded that the quality of service is then directly tied to the amount of male and female representation within an organization. Both common sense and research support this to be true. And this is one tenet of the value of diversity. Certainly, there are a great many businesses that have benefitted from that position and practice and many that have suffered by not practicing such. On the surface, this too may appear a simple numbers practice, that of targeting the *number* of male and female representatives to those represented and serviced based on gender demographics. That then makes it appear to be a numbers-centric solution. But here again, numbers are just part of the problem, so numbers can be only a partial solution. As has been said all along, imbalance or balance can transcend the numbers. If we consider more deeply the principle of representation, it's not just having representatives in one's corner but more a matter of having representatives actively working on one's behalf. Presence alone does little good. To truly represent one's customers, clients, and stakeholders, representatives have to *do* things. Representatives have to be empowered to contribute and influence upon one's behalf. Which brings us right back to our definition of balance. When an organization enables female and male staff to act, make decisions, and promote on behalf of those it serves, the organization can succeed in its service. Without fully enabling empowered representation by both men and women, an organization truly abandons the principles of customer service and suffers detrimental consequences to its success.

- **Bias.** Consider that no man or no woman is free of bias. When one gender dominates, its interests dominate. Studies show that men fight harder for scarce resources, for example. Thus, in male-dominated organizations, male interests are more strongly served. Bias can skew how customers, clients, and stakeholders are served and actually who those customers, clients, and stakeholders might be. For example, in a gender-imbalanced organization, product development is determined by the dominant gender. In a scientific organization, as another example, the targeted research is determined, resourced, and carried out by the dominant gender. Because most scientific organizations are male-dominant, male bias persists in the targeting and focus of scientific pursuit. And when it comes to research selection, filtering and exclusion of scientific data itself also takes place. This is a big deal. Consider such effects as product discrimination or even scientific integrity. Male-centeredness (androcentrism) may preclude sex differences from being considered. Imagine such bias when it comes to drug testing or cancer research, for example. Lest you think it wouldn't happen, early car crash dummies were all male. As a result, initial testing of seatbelts and airbags ignored things such as pregnancy. Male dominance in the industry also led to women being killed by first-generation airbags at speeds of only 20 mph because they didn't foresee that breasts close to the steering wheel could force the airbags upward. In reproduction studies, androcentric research saw the sperm as the only active component and discounted activity of the female reproductive system; the sperm was anointed the "active" component and the egg "passive." Late in study, gender bias was overcome to allow the identification and recognition that the egg has finger-like projections (microvilli) that grab sperm and pull them in. Oftentimes, gendered bias goes unnoticed until more balance is realized. Of course, imbalance could be the other way around—gynocentric. Examples of female bias exist as well. Yet another form of bias in an unbalanced organization is the minority trying not to appear to pander to their sex. Women scientists originally shied away from studying primate pregnancy and primate infants, for example, because it could have been seen as giving in to feminine bias by doing so. Much can be done to neutralize such biases, and those things are exactly what is being prescribed here—parity in contribution and influence.

- **Groupthink.** Another consequence of homogenous groups is groupthink. Groupthink is overzealous interest in reaching consensus in meetings. By overzealous I mean putting the goal of consensus over good outcomes. This occurs largely as a matter of conformity. The more homogenous/nondiverse a group is, the more easily it slips into groupthink.

- **Performance.** Performance is truly a last-but-not-least concern. In imbalanced and nondiverse environments, organizational performance is not only hindered, but it is placed or kept on an ever declining path in relation to better-balanced and better-performing organizations. Studies show that well-managed, diverse teams outperform homogeneous teams by up to six times. In other words, imbalanced organizations are likely being outpaced by more diverse and balanced organizations by that same figure. Diverse and balanced organizations pass, pull away from, and leave nondiverse and imbalanced organizations in their dust. At the beginning of this chapter, I cited statistical evidence attesting to the positive effects of gender balance on performance. Much of that ties to the fact that imbalanced organizations do not value all the skills and knowledge available to them and, thus, are not fully leveraged. Furthermore, contribution and influence are hampered on a personal level and, as a result, affect individual performance. We can reiterate how lack of representation affects organizational performance, and so on. All issues of gender imbalance are issues of (under)performance. Lack of attendance to the former results in lack of the latter.

Perhaps with the exception of performance, the items above might be seen as purely a numbers issue—balance in terms of ratios and diversity. But again, that is only the surface view. As we continue to look deeper, it will become more evident that balance is more about power and influence.

A thousand examples could be listed to argue that gender balance is worthy of focused organizational attention. Balance is tied directly to organizational well-being. Were an imbalanced company to ignore taking steps toward better balance, the consequences cut to the core of what most leaders hold dear—the very success of the organization.

Everyone loses in imbalanced organizations.

Chapter 4

Gender Balance

One way to visualize the problem (and solutions) of gender balance would be to think of an old-fashioned weighing scale. Picture one side loaded with heavy blue marbles and the other side with far fewer pink marbles. The seemingly obvious cause of the unbalanced scale is the amount of weight on either side, and it follows that the obvious solution is to add weight to the pink side or take away weight from the blue side.

But there are actually three ways to improve balance.

1. Adjust the quantity. Change the numbers of marbles to more a more balanced ratio

2. Manually manipulate the scales.

3. Adjust the weight (value). Rather than changing the number of marbles on either side, increase of weight of those already present—increase one's value.

Numbered vs. Non-numbered Balancing

Let's consider numbers first. Balance and gender disparity could simply be a matter of numbers. And that can be addressed with a numbers solution. Those solutions include recruiting, hiring, retention, and promotion.

A strong case can be made that the ratio of men and women in an organization is what drives balance. For example, women have been found to receive lower ratings when they are less than 20% of a group.

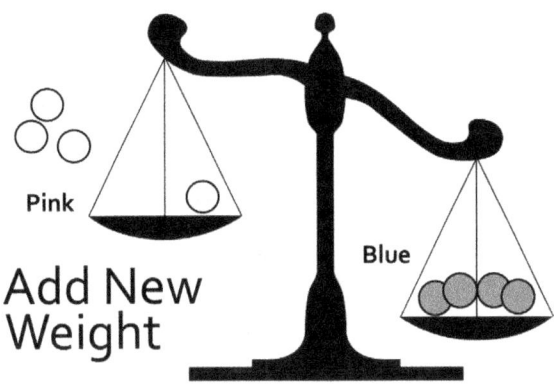

From this, one can see the connection between numbered representation and the statistics cited on evaluations. It seems apparent that there is a direct and very solid connection. The argument is thus that ratings would improve with more balanced numbers.

The rule of three offers similar evidence. The rule of three states that the opinion of a woman on a board is given less weight than a man's until there are three women on that board. Change the composition and things start changing. And they may change quickly.

But the answer is not so simple. Women tend to withdraw from groups in which men exercise power-assertive behaviors. And it's no secret that numbers are power. However, that power is not exclusive to the numbers themselves. And so, the cause is not exclusively numbers-bound, nor are the solutions. Through purposeful measures and actuating systems, it is possible to give more weight to everyone. Numbers and balance are thus not inextricably connected.

Advances toward balance can be had regardless of numerical changes.

Consider the following example. Research has found that when women are included in groups in any numbers, the collective intelligence is higher than with men alone, regardless of the individual intelligence of members.[32] Again, on the surface this looks like another case that numbers dictate affect. But note that the research said, "in any numbers." The ratio matters far less than the initial impact of inserting gender diversity. The insertion adds value not previously there.

Likewise, let's challenge another assumption. A 2018 study by the

University of Kent in the UK found the assumption that female-dominated workplaces are better at providing gender-friendly programs and practices to be false. Researchers found that women in female-dominated workplaces have less access to flexible working arrangements than those in gender-neutral, gender-balanced, and even male-dominated offices. The study found the best places for providing flexibility and accommodation are gender-neutral or gender-balanced.

There are many instances where the assumption is not true that balancing the numbers will result in true organizational gender balance, where men and women have real parity.

To clarify, let's look once again at gender balance from an organizational standpoint. Just because an organization has women staff in equal, near equal, or greater numbers than men does not mean it is balanced. Even if the staffing up and down the entirety of an organization's hierarchy is relatively equal, there could still be imbalance. In fact, no ratio of men to women necessarily makes an organization more or less balanced as defined here. And by the same token, any uneven ratio of men and women in an organization does not necessarily make that organization imbalanced.

Experiential Background in Imbalance

Let me give just a bit of my background that lead me to these conclusions. A significant chunk of my career was spent doing instruction and diversity work for a large government agency—one that was extremely unbalanced in terms of both male-to-female ratio and fully inclusive involvement in all processes. Of the former, some of the imbalance could be attributed to the agency being a scientific one—there was a natural shortage of women in the agency because of the shortage of women in STEM in general. But that was only partial cause. The other could be attributed to the self-perpetuating nature of the unbalanced ratio and its direct correlation to recruiting and retention. The former opened my eyes to the latter.

During my many years with this organization, I was steeped in diversity and inclusion efforts, much of which focused on various issues of gender. I was chair of the agency's national diversity council as well as a diversity ambassador representing the issues and interests of LGBTQIA individuals and women. I was a leading member of a gender focus working group that worked on internal gender issues (e.g., staffing, empowerment, awareness, education, etc.), external issues (gender-sensitive products and services, gender equality and gender mainstreaming policy, practices, education, etc.) with international partner organizations.

Through the years, what I and my colleagues struggled with most was recruiting and retention. Despite numerous and varied efforts, we just could not make headway in improving the numbers of women in the organization. This, in turn, had additional negative effects on the number of women attaining higher ranks in the organization. At a point in these efforts, I experienced a revelation of sorts. I realized we were not only losing the battle we were fighting, but we were fighting the wrong battle. The goal we were trying to attain was a rightful goal, but it was not the ultimate goal.

The numbers goal was not the end. Rather, it was one means, one step, toward the ultimate goal—gender parity in contribution and influence within the organization.

So, my work began anew with a different focus—an additional way to balance the organization.

That is not to say that equal or near equal representation is not important to an organization. In saying that gender-balanced organizations outperform imbalanced organizations, gender balance could very well be evidenced in terms of numbers. Numbers are an obvious indicator—but they are just one indicator. Numbers can also be a solution to imbalance, but again that is but one solution. The numbers are an indicator and a tool. Mostly they are a starting point—the means to an end. Again, they are a step toward the ultimate goal of equity in inclusion, contribution, influence and voice. Those things can be a result of equitable numbers of female and male employees in an organization, but where a numbers inequality exists there are other means to advance equity.

Before setting aside consideration of numbers, let me be clear that balancing numbers is a good thing. Bettering the numbers is a direct route to our goal. This book will discuss numbers options (e.g., recruiting, retention) later, but much more time will be given to non-numbers-bound solutions.

Defining Balance

An analogy may help clarify a new definition of balance—a sports analogy.

Suppose you owned a professional sports franchise with a persistent losing record. That could be attributed to a bad ratio of poor to good players—or more specifically to the number of good players. As the club owner, you could try to resolve the team's performance by acquiring better players through money, trades, or the draft. That can be seen as a numbers solution to a numbers problem. But is the problem as simple as it appears? Is it all about the number of perceived good players and bad players? Or could it be more a matter of the current group of players' potential being accessed, which might more appropriately be addressed by better coaching of skills and motivation. It may be that the environment and/or systems being used are not well tuned or are out of sync with the players on hand. There can be many reasons for players underperforming and/or not fully contributing. Recognizing and acknowledging those reasons can identify solutions to achieve better performance with players already on the team. The makeup of the team, while not inconsequential, is less important than fully tapping into and using the potential of the current members through systems and practices.

As noted previously, successful teams have these three characteristics:

1. **Social sensitivity.** This is awareness of and empathy for others. Awareness has been a huge component of what I have taught teams and leaders. It allows us to adjust appropriately to the needs of the people we serve, and that includes internal staff and employees. Teams thrive when they are cognizant of the needs of others and respond appropriately. Empathy is the ability to be aware on a deep level, to see things not only through your eyes and perspective but more importantly through the eyes and perspectives of others and to have a real appreciation of others' perspectives. Again, this allows for appropriate service and accommodation, and in the bigger picture, it allows for things like the more effective relational approach or leadership

style. One thing to point out here is that awareness and empathy are skills both men and women possess. But more women possess these skills to begin with, and they possess them to higher, more practiced levels. Hold that thought for item 3.

2. **Equal contribution.** This goes right to the heart of the position fostered in this book. The definition of gender balance is parity in contribution and influence. In the end, it is not only equal contribution but maximum contribution as derived from an environment that allows everyone, men and women, to fully contribute. Much more will be said on this in the coming pages.

3. **More women.** On the surface it looks like a numbers issue. But as will be discussed later, it is rather a matter of a better balance in terms of what is brought to the table. It may sound like the solution is to add women, but really what is being said is to add more diverse traits (especially feminine traits). Most organizations are male-dominated and thus homogeneous not only in terms of sex but also in terms of traits and skills utilized, approaches and methods, communication and leadership styles, and so on. Adding women makes more offices simply more diverse on more than one level. Returning to item 1, for example, adding women can insert more awareness and empathy. Again, I will expand upon this in another chapter.

When we look for solutions that will gain a better balance and all the rewards that come with it, we must look beyond simply adding women to organizations. Instead, organizational processes need to be reshaped to create the space for women's and men's equitable and appropriate involvement.

By processes, I mean any organizational activity in which there is personal involvement, participation, contribution, and influence by individuals—that is, *all* activities of the organization. One example is meetings. You are probably familiar with the phrase *seat at the table*. In a literal sense, when it comes to adding women to a process such as a meeting, a seat at the table means simply inviting more women to meetings.

Space and Participation

I like to use seat-at-the-table examples often in teaching this topic. The terminology can be taken figuratively, analogously, or literally. Literally, a seat at the table could mean a seat at a meeting room table or on a conference panel. It could also mean being one of a slate of speakers at a conference or a board member, member of some team, contributor to a policy, tester, reviewer or author. It's anywhere an underrepresented individual may need to be provided space.

A seat at the table also implies providing voice. A seat at the table does not produce balance if it is not a seat of participation. That holds true for whatever process might be considered. *Voice* is another good term to use because high-profile articles are more often written by men, lecterns are more spoken from by men, and boardrooms are filled with a disproportionate number of male voices. At the majority of conferences most keynote speakers are men. Panels are so frequently all-male that a new word evolved to describe the phenomenon: *manels*. News stories are reported more by men by a huge margin, and this imbalance is reflected in how infrequently women are quoted in news stories. And only 9% of contributors on Wikipedia are women.[33] Even though women make up half the population, women's voices have been historically quiet or entirely absent in public spaces. These imbalances cause lack of participation and influence and ultimately deny leadership opportunities to women.

What counts is participation, not appearances. Another word for participation that is too often and too quickly diluted of its true meaning is *inclusion*. Inclusion, as it pertains to gender, can be defined as ensuring both men and women enjoy involvement in all processes fully and equitably. Inclusion means not only bringing people into a body but bringing them into participation. Presence and participation give value to all a person has to offer (knowledge, perspective, skills, talents, personality, culture, etc.).

Inclusion describes our goal accurately. Yet, I like to return to the word *balance*. To my mind, balance implies more of an anticipatable goal. It implies an attainable state. Balance means gender parity in contribution and influence. It's empowerment—a state of empowerment and one not bounded by numbers.

In the big picture, balance is about the whole of the environment that breeds and sustains the processes that open up space at the table. Thus, it's about creating an environment where all (in equal fashion) are empowered, enabled to give the best they have, enabled to influence outcomes and recognized and valued. Recognition and value are applied to both potential (a person's inherent and learned traits and skills) and to performance.

Contribution and Influence Parity

I've defined equality and inclusion and danced around a definition of balance. Now I can say in straightforward fashion that *balance* is contribution and influence parity.

Parity, of course, implies equality, but I will argue it's not always equal. And I'll argue that in actuality, when it comes to balance, parity is *seldom* equal.

This definition of balance fits right in with a broader, globally embraced definition and is actually measurable. The United Nations defines empowerment in measurable terms. The Gender Empowerment Measure examines the extent to which women and men are able to actively participate in economic and political life and take part in decision-making. Participation and decision-making are key to measuring empowerment, which can be legitimately tied to increased value. *Participation* is another word for *contribution*, and *decision-making* is another word for *influence*. The definition of balance—that of parity in contribution and influence—then holds true and can be a measurable goal.

So, what do measurable participation and decision-making look like? What is contribution and influence parity or, as this next example notes, contribution and influence *disparity*?

A recent study found that women who were equally competent to men were consulted on important decisions three times less often than men.

You might think that parity as a principal component of balance would suggest that women ought to be consulted in an exactly equal number of occurrences as men. We can hold that up as an ideal, but gender balance allows for parity in contribution and influence to be more flexible. It is not, and need not be, fixed on some kind of 50/50 standard. Rather we should look at parity as a matter of *more*. We would want women to be consulted *more*—much more as a matter of everyday practice. The goal would be, for example, that such workplace practices as decision-consulting of women is *more* on par with decision-consulting of men within in the course of a day, week, month, or year, and regardless of the numbers of men and women.

It might also be a good time to remember that gender means both men and women. While studies do indicate women are consulted less in most workplaces and spheres, it is entirely possible, and likely does exist in places, that men are in a position of minority in an organization and might then be in a lesser position of influence. Ultimately, gender balance is about *more* for all. It's finding ways to get *more* contribution from men and women, though especially from the underrepresented and disadvantaged.

The ideal would be that *more* is so well pursued that equal need not be a consideration or a goal but rather a more free-flowing natural outcome.

That ideal requires continuous cognizant attention. All people in an organization need always to be aware of balance or imbalance. They need to be observant of the numbers of men and women involved in workplace processes. Here again the key is awareness of involvement more than awareness of presence.

Again, this is not simply a numbers issue. Just because the women in an organization may be only, say, 25%, that does not mean lectern time should likewise be aligned with that number. Rather it should be *more* balanced. Being in any position of influence or contribution should be a matter of parity. That doesn't mean representation should always be 50/50 or even close to it, necessarily, but the goal is to lean toward balance and not be numbers-bound. It's not about simply adding people to the room; rather, it's providing more seats at the table where contribution can occur. The same holds true in the equitable leading of meetings, being on or leading teams, being published, or working key assignments. Better balance means parity in men's and women's involvement in processes and outcomes. It is a power balance more so than a numbers balance.

By now I hope I have made clear that balance it is not a matter of numbers but more so effect. With voice, for example, there are tangible consequences to the lack thereof. Voice is visibility. Visibility is influence, and visibility also creates opportunity. Imbalance then is, as but one example, a matter of opportunity inequity. This in turn may yield authority inequity and that, in turn, can lead to potentially positional inequality and so on. The seemingly minor hindrances to voice and participation have huge ramifications in the big picture and over the long haul. Those hindrances can have very personal ramifications as well. Inequities such as disparate participative opportunities hinder an individual's ability to develop and grow, to succeed, and to advance in an organization. It is not a stretch to say that the lack of lectern time or the inability to fully participate in meetings, for example, may directly result in a hampered career where potential is unrealized.

Balance is also more discreetly a matter of female inclusion and empowerment (or male inclusion and empowerment wherever men might be the undervalued and/or disadvantaged). How much women, or men, are allowed and empowered to contribute and influence is the real measurement of balance.

With numbers-bound solutions, the issue was adding marbles (women or men) to one side or another of the scale. With non-numbers-bound solutions, the issue is adding value to the underrepresented to increase their presence. It is creating a leveled environment and reshaping processes to create the space for women's and men's equitable and appropriate involvement. It is creating an environment where all in equal fashion are enabled to give the best they have. And it is about empowering undervalued individuals to increase their value. In being so enabled people can fully contribute and influence the outcomes. In this type of environment both the contributors and their contributions are recognized and valued in all their diverse forms.

Rather than option 1 (number of marbles) to better balance the scale, which is the most typical approach, an organization could put more focus on option 2 (manipulation) or option 3 (adding weight/value to what is already present).

Balance via the Five Fingers of Manipulation

Option 2 is a good place to start. It is tipping—er, righting the scales in the interest of balance. In a sense it is manual manipulation as opposed to quantity adjustment, at least in keeping with our scale analogy. Rather than adjusting the weights, what if we (the organization) simply leveled it with our (imaginary) hand? That is exactly what many

Manipulate the scale

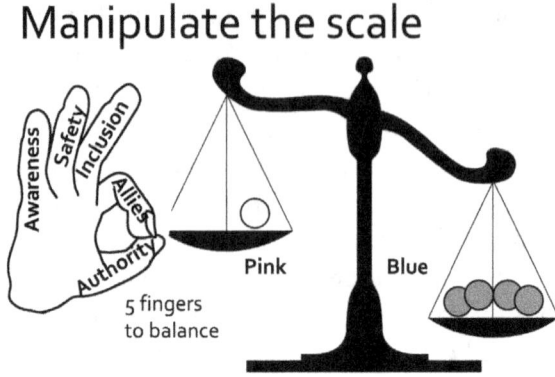

organizations need to do. They could manually and actively tip the scales through actions.

The specific elements needed to create an environment of better balance fall into five mandatory categories, or actions:

- **Awareness.** Awareness of gender issues and biases throughout the organization.

- **Security.** Safe, respectful, accommodating, and supportive environment where all are respected and valued, and everyone is free from harassment of any type.

- **Inclusion.** An inclusive environment that makes space for all to participate with all they have to bring to the table and all traits, skills, methods, techniques, knowledge, perspective, and experiences valued.

- **Allies.** Allies who are empathetic and supportive. These come in many forms, but regardless of form, they fulfill a lifting need in one way or another.

- **Authority.** Balance by decree. Leadership taking responsibility, ownership, and dictating balance formally and vocally. Giving credibility to the principle and weight to leveling processes.

And let's call these five categories the five fingers of manipulation. They are means to manually tip the scales.

The five fingers operate together, with each dependent upon the others. You cannot really achieve any one of these fully unless you achieve them all. Each requires a level of organizational ownership of real solutions that puts systems, procedures, policies, plans, and practices in place to support all five.

Let's start with awareness, not because it's listed first, but more because it's a prerequisite to everything else. Without awareness, problems cannot be identified and addressed.

Security has to be the next priority. In truth it should be first as a matter of personal importance. But security can't be made to happen if people don't recognize the problem. Initial awareness efforts can and should focus on personal safety. If employees don't feel safe from harm, they are unable to participate and contribute fully. It is impossible to be included and empowered when you feel unsafe. Furthermore, humans need safety and nutrients of many forms to thrive. Where organizations fall short in this, people wither or leave. These are often the people organizations rely upon. Imbalance cannot be realized where people feel unsettled.

Once employees feel safe and their needs are accommodated, organizations can turn attention to ensuring all employees are fully included. Though the term *inclusion* has been around a good many years, it has of late rightfully taken over airspace previously occupied by *tolerance*. Inclusion as a concept is more powerful and appropriate than tolerance. Inclusion is about active participation, while tolerance is passive. And as a matter of active participation, inclusion is aligned well with the concept of balance. The problem is that inclusion may be widely talked about and even generally understood, but it is not truly practiced, or it is practiced inappropriately.

Once a secure and nurturing environment is established and people are added to processes in an inclusive and (more) balanced fashion, parity in contribution and influence is ultimately achieved by maximizing and capitalizing on the human value. That goes beyond being inclusive of people to being inclusive of all a person has to give (traits, skills, perspectives, knowledge, etc.).

The fourth finger is allies. Allies are needed to assist where anyone is disadvantaged. Allies could be seen as part of all the previous items. For example, allies are means to a safer environment, means of awareness, and means to empowerment. The same could be said of awareness, though. The point being is that there is much integration of mechanisms of balance. It matters little if you see allies as a separate piece or not; the important thing here is that all the pieces are accounted for.

And the fifth and final finger is authority or, as I sometimes call it, balance by decree. While leadership can be actively involved in any or all of the other four requirements, balance won't be achieved or gain buy-in without obvious leadership proclamation and ownership. Merely saying "Go balance" cannot make it so, but not saying it will make it a certain failure. Leaders can do many things to decree balance, but the rest of the hand, the other four fingers, must also be done.

Increasing Weight (Value) through Empowerment

Getting back to our scale, recall that option 3 for balancing was to increase the weight (value) of the weights already present on the lesser side. That certainly is doable. Raising one's value is in large part a matter of empowerment—both organizational empowerment and self-empowerment. Balance can be vastly improved by empowering processes.

When we increase the weight of what already exists, what we are really doing is giving what is already there more value. Value allows for both using a person's unique abilities and enhancing those abilities. But it goes beyond raising ability to expanding capacity. Capacity implies an unboundedness. It allows for not only increase but also broadening, adaption, and evolution. This is how a person's value can truly be increased and maximized.

Empowerment (programs, activities, and practices that raise value and capacity) should be seen as an absolute necessity in imbalanced workplaces. The further value is raised and capacity expanded, the more contribution and influence can be maximized.

Think of it as balancing the scale not with quantity but with quality, as increasing the weight of what is already present versus adding new weight.

Increasing quality is not exclusively focused on raising the value of one side over the other. Rather, raising value of anyone raises the value of everyone. An increase on one side does not represent a decrease on the other.

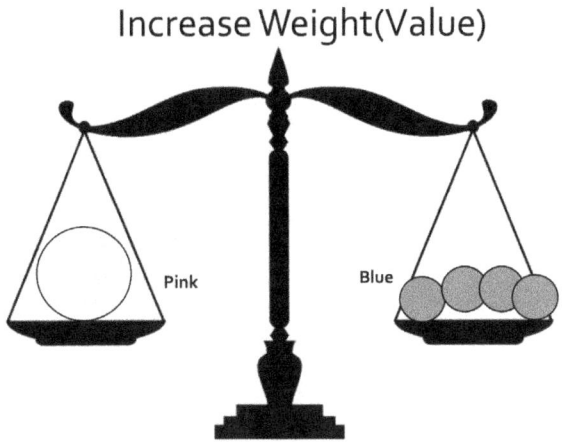

Summary

Given our definition of balance as contribution and influence parity, we have identified three means of achieving balance. Two of those means required no weight or number alteration. Rather, we could manually manipulate with the five fingers, or we could increase the weight (value) of what already exists. In going forth we will give more attention to options 2 and 3. These options are especially promising for organizations that have struggled with the numbers.

Again, I am not saying that leveling by numbers is not important or that leveling by numbers does not work. They are important strategies, and they can work as one possible solution. However, numbers solutions are not always possible, practical, or even optimal, and they are not necessary. That does not mean that recruiting, hiring, and retention won't be discussed (they will).

None of these solutions is easy. In the end, addressing balance through processes and systems that foster contribution and influence parity requires vision, a new mindset, and culture change.

Chapter 5

Awareness

People need reasons to change and reasons to act. People will not embrace anti-harassment programs or seat-at-the-table programs or empowerment programs or gender balance programs of any type of program unless they can first see the need for and benefit of those programs.

- The greater men's awareness of gender bias, the more likely they are to feel it is important to achieve gender equality.[34]
- Men with a high awareness of gender bias were more likely to view women's workplace exclusion as a competitive disadvantage for corporations.[35]
- About 65% of women polled say their gender faces at least some discrimination, while only 48% of men believe it exists. Only 10% of men believed their own workplaces treated women unfairly.[36]
- Seventy-seven percent of women feel there is gender inequality in the workplace, compared to 56% of men.[37]
- Both McKinsey and Lean In found that women question overall issues of general fairness in the workplace much more frequently than men do. Not only did a full third of women surveyed believe their gender makes it harder to get a promotion, raise, or generally get ahead at work (compared to 12% of men), but less than half (44%) of female respondents thought

the best opportunities went to the most deserving employees (compared to 54% of male respondents).[38]

- A survey by PwC showed mixed enthusiasm about addressing inequities among executive leaders. As reported by NBC News, "58 percent of male directors surveyed think efforts are driven by political correctness, compared to 27 percent of female directors. Around 54 percent of male directors think shareholders are too preoccupied with the subject, compared to just 20 percent of female directors."[39]

- A 2019 report by Chief Executive Women and Bain and Company illuminated that there is a huge "perception gap" between men and women when it comes to the promotion of gender equality.[40] It revealed not only the extent to which men think they are already doing "enough" but also what men think would have the greatest impact. Men and women are simply not talking about the same thing, even when they think they are. The majority of men (64%) already think they're doing a great job, while the majority of women (70%) think men need to do more.

Edification

To resolve organizational gender issues, there must be acknowledgment of the problems, understanding of the problems, and understanding of the benefits of solutions. While this should include everyone in an organization, it must at least include organizational leadership. Gender sensitivity should be a required core competency and an evaluation metric. Awareness training should be offered, encouraged, and mandated.

To begin, organizational leadership must take ownership of the issues by understanding them, and not simply defer or delegate responsibility to others to become informed.

I have two recommendations to start with.

1. **Begin gender dialog.** Recognize and talk about gender as a facet of workplace performance and relationships. If you are a leader, ensure gender conversations and communications take place,

and invite staff and employees into the conversation. At meetings, insert gender as an agenda topic, especially in policy and program planning meetings. See to it that gender is included in training and conferences. If you are an employee, make sure others and management know that gender warrants discussion. Don't shy away from open discussion of the topic, whether in the boardroom or the breakroom. Have evidence on hand of the ramifications of balance, imbalance, and gender implications in the workplace. Share everywhere and with everyone you can. Use internal social media to share gender information. Work toward identifying allies and champions and means of more formal education.

2. **Research and document.** Increase your own knowledge. Research gender from many sources, and find evidence of its workplace impacts to share with others. Keep your eyes and ears open for media stories to save, share, and post. Become a source of gender information, and let others know you as a source. Join social media and other groups where gender is a focus. Build a knowledge bank of gender information. Gather and share gender best practices. Document and share success stories and other evidence of improved performance brought about by improved balance.

To become informed, you must do your homework. Study the data. Just as a company with a reputation as a leader in product innovation would want to determine how they can most successfully launch new products, a company that aspires to be more inclusive should look at its numbers around recruitment, retention, engagement, and promotion.

If women are being hired at entry level at the same rate as men, but few of them reach senior positions, that might suggest that women are given fewer opportunities for advancement than men. If the pipeline narrows above manager, dig into what discrepancies and systemic issues may exist.

If you suspect a pay gap between men and women, simply ask HR for the data.

If you discover that women are leaving because they are unsure about their career trajectories, you may want to dig into talent-development processes, including sponsorship and communications.

If women are leaving, you'll want to know where they are going and why. Did they think they wouldn't get promoted? Did they get training and mentoring? How do the numbers look over time, and what are the factors driving these results? That's how you figure out your response.

Numbers never tell the whole story. Leaders should also tap into engagement surveys, focus groups, and exit interviews for feedback on people's experiences, as well as the impact of specific policies.

The most common approach to diversity and inclusion awareness is to, in a sense, shed off responsibility onto others. In so doing, leaders not only absolve much responsibility, but they also fail in ascertaining any real effectiveness. Diversity and inclusion awareness is largely a check-box exercise in too many organizations.

One example is the cultural lunch. I call this "spring roll" diversity. I don't mean to demean spring rolls or the culture they are associated with, and in fact, I encourage these types of events. Lunches can encourage awareness of what is unique and wonderful about people, but that doesn't necessarily make them a good tool compared to better tools. Inclusion is far more than inviting someone to share a native dish. But checking boxes is easier than using better tools. While these lunches do move the needle some in terms of acceptance, they don't raise the type of awareness that is being discussed here. The type of awareness that is needed identifies issues, concerns, sheds light on value, identifies and opens doors to solutions, and so on.

Sharing snippets of information with others through lunches, posters, newsletters, and the like can help, but only in small increments. To get more benefit, however, any such activity can be broadened to raise awareness on a larger scale.

Information Campaigns

Specific informative campaigns can be temporary or permanent features of the workplace. For example, a workgroup could have a poster design contest or hang posters that highlight gender issues. Office or factory newsletters can publish articles about gender. Another idea is sanctioned observance days in which members of a workplace or workgroup dress in a specific color for the day These can be tied to national movements like #MeToo or #TimeIsUp. Movements like #MeToo have been boons in raising awareness, and can thus be leveraged.

HeForShe, as example, has been astonishing as a tool of awareness. It is also a globally recognized call for action for all of the world's women and men on behalf of women everywhere. A big part of that is to make men agents of change in tackling inequalities, or allies, which will be discussed in full later in this book.

These campaigns can be a great time for gender champions (also to be discussed in detail in a later chapter) to make pledges or commitments. Here's an example.

As a gender champion, I pledge to:

- Review and understand all EEO-related policies regarding gender equality.
- Make it known to all that I am a gender champion.
- Be open to discussing any gender issues in the workplace.
- Thoroughly educate myself on gender issues in the workplace.
- Help educate my staff about gender issues in the workplace.
- Be a catalyst for gender-sensitive practices.
- Equitably increase opportunities for empowerment of all genders.
- Insert gender equality into meeting agendas.
- Recruit others to commit to championing gender equality.
- Create space for belittled voices.
- Open more seats at the table for the underrepresented.

These are just a few examples of pledges.

Organizational leaders can also demonstrate their commitment to gender parity through videos or written statements. I have always believed that personal stories are the most powerful and most effective way to reach a person and affect their thoughts. When leaders or others share stories about personal harms and personal realizations, others listen, often empathetically. When the heart is reached, the mind is opened.

This takes some vulnerability on behalf of leaders, but I see it as more investment than risk. Giving is always a prerequisite to reaping. Leaders need to put themselves out there with resonating messages that complement information. The more an executive is personally open about their motivations and their story, the more powerful the message.

The best of these are videotaped statements that are distributed across an entire organization. Video adds the power of personalization. But these days there is no shortage of ways to get messages out there.

Social media has been a boon to information dissemination on just about every subject. Gender in the workplace is no exception. I have seen podcasts used effectively in confined workgroups or organizations, and I have seen hosted panel discussions on the subject of gender that have been recorded and disseminated within organizations. There is no limit to how a group can imaginatively use social media to raise awareness.

Recall the story I told about my mother and her non-Hillary vote. The issue was not being able to *see* a woman president. Awareness is often a matter of visibility. In a latter chapter, the value of role models will be looked at more closely, but here understand that role models are also tools of awareness. When people see female CFOs, female captains, female engineers, and female presidents, they become informed of possibilities. And likewise for male caregivers, for example. Minds are opened up to seeing gender capabilities more expansively. Visible role models can be every bit as powerful as personal stories.

Role models can be made central components of awareness campaigns. One agency I worked for did just that, and in multiple ways. For example, they had a website highlighting "Women of…"—women of engineering, women of leadership, women in the field, etc. In this same agency there was a rather famous leader, a former astronaut, whose notoriety aided her visibility. She was a role model to be sure, but she also was vocal and used personal stories in increase awareness.

Broad campaigns can include an array of these tools and may include permanent fixtures, such as a dedicated website.

Informational Groups

Employee resource groups (aka ERGs or affinity groups) support and represent specific groups, such as women. Their role in the workplace is to support people in their target group, make their workplace experience better, and assist them in their careers. ERGs can provide resources, but for my money what they can also offer—which is just as valuable as any other resource—is information. This can be information that is useful to the targeted group but also, and just as importantly, information *about* the targeted group. Such shared information serves as advocation. It is not a stretch to see that ERGs function as champions in their own way.

If an organization doesn't already have any programs in place that are focused on and active in supporting, advocating, or helping women, then creating an ERG is a great option as a starting point.

In my career I lead a women's affinity group. While we did many things to help the women in our organization, the piece that was easiest to implement, and thus arguably the most effective, was informational activities. These included newsletter articles, poster campaigns, webinars, and so on. I can state unequivocally that through these efforts we raised awareness (and much more).

Structured information also has its place largely in the form of training. Gender awareness is greatly imparted through formal training in topics such as anti-harassment, unconscious bias, and cross-skills training.

Awareness Training

Organizations should also conduct or host gender training.

Soft-skills training, which is likely already being conducted in most workplaces, can and should include elements of gender. And organizations should make gender-awareness training available to as many employees as possible in whatever forms feasible. If an organization truly desires balance, it must understand that balance does not rest solely in the hands of leaders and managers. Balance involves everyone. All employees should understand the environmental and cultural situation, the role gender plays, implications to the organization, and the value and means of balance.

All-hands education should be conducted to raise gender IQ. Again, this might include classes or webinars on the topic of gender balance, sexual harassment (laws, awareness, prevention, bystanders), unconscious/implicit bias, empowerment, and cross-gender skills training.

In 2018 Starbucks made a powerful example of education and corporate message through corporate-wide training on unconscious bias. The training was precipitated by an incident in which two black men were kicked out of a Philadelphia Starbucks store and arrested because they were in the store but hadn't ordered anything. While some people saw Starbucks' response as pure public relations, it did, at a minimum, raise awareness of the issue. And it wasn't only optics. Starbucks legitimately wanted to educate its staff nationwide. The training was accomplished at *great* cost to the company. Such commitment should serve as example to other organizations.

When I conduct gender awareness training, I often lead off with correcting these myths of gender equality:

1. **Myth:** Gender equality benefits some at the cost of others.
   Truth: Gender equality is not a win-lose proposition. Despite an unfortunate and all too common erroneous belief, one gender does not win at the cost of the other side losing. Equality, in any form as applied to any group, is not a fixed pie from which people have to wrest their fair share. I don't like any pie analogy because it is an entirely wrong image. It presents equality as a consumable rather than a dividend. If you insist on using a food analogy, how about fruit? Equality could be considered fruit—the more that is grown, the more seeds are available for further growth and expansion. Equality can be grown and nurtured. As fruit, it can be said to be consumed in a sense, but the benefits of consumption are growth. Rather than cutting back on anything, the seeds, as both source and product of growth, perpetuate and expand the fruit to the benefit of more and more people. Ultimately, equality is not a matter of fixed, static or status, but is truly a matter of expansion—more!

2. **Myth:** Gender equality is about the advancement of women's issues.
   Truth: Gender equality, as a growth-based apparatus, is win-win and not win-lose. And win-win applies to all. It is not an

issue of women alone. Rather, the win is for men and women, people of both genders. It has positive effects on all individuals. It is actually a win-win in perpetuity because winning extends to groups, organizations, and society itself—a universal win. Some may staunchly hold the skewed belief that when others lose they win, but such belief is self-centered and delusional. All the evidence supports that everyone, men and women alike, benefits from gender equality. Truly, the rising tide raises the ship for all aboard.

3. **Myth:** Gender equality is all about equal numbers.
Truth: Gender equality is about strength and power. It is about being on strong and equal footing in relationships with others regardless of gender, it is about social and economic power on par with others of any gender, and it is about having authority in decision-making with equal weight as any other person. Gender equality is a very expansive principle—a principle, not an equation.

Though not specific to gender, unconscious bias training is a must. This solution to bias has received much attention as of late, and very rightfully so. The concept of unconscious bias, also known as implicit bias, is, in a nutshell, that we all have biases we simply don't have a conscious awareness of. These biases often take the form of implicit associations we have concerning types or groups of people. For example, we may have a sense that a certain group of people (be it a cultural grouping, age, or whatever) is lazy. We may not really give it conscious consideration; we just internally assume it so. And we may act based on these biases without being aware of the unconscious motivations to our behaviors. These associations do not necessarily align with our declared beliefs or even reflect stances we would explicitly endorse.

Implicit biases are malleable. Our brains are incredibly complex, and the implicit associations that we have formed can be gradually unlearned through a variety of debiasing techniques. Unconscious bias training can both identify what these biases and associations may be and train our consciousness to break these associations, thus tempering prejudice and inappropriate behavior.

Gender Mainstreaming as an Awareness Tool

A very structured, broad, and strong-armed approach to overall gender balance is gender mainstreaming. This is a common term and concept among international organizations, but it is less known in America. The intent of gender mainstreaming is to instill gender sensitivities in all decision processes.

By definition, gender mainstreaming is the process for assessing the implications for women and men of any planned action, including legislation, policies, or programs, in all areas and at all levels. It is a strategy for making women's, as well as men's, concerns and experiences an integral dimension of the design, implementation, monitoring, and evaluation of policies and programs in all political, economic, and societal spheres so that women and men benefit equally, and inequality is not perpetuated.

Gender mainstreaming is in a sense a tool to achieve gender balance in and of itself. I have worked on gender mainstreaming with global organizations, including contributing to policy, programs, education, and more. As a member of the World Meteorological Organization's panel of experts on gender mainstreaming, I witnessed firsthand how gender mainstreaming works as a tool of change—a mechanism of gender balance.

Gender mainstreaming is a lot of things, but for my money, its greatest worth is that of a lens—a gender-awareness or gender-sensitive lens.

It puts concentrated focus on gender as a facet of people's experiences to the exclusion of other facets. There can be other forms of mainstreaming (race, culture, economic, disability, etc.), but gender mainstreaming is obviously most relevant as a tool of gender balance.

Gender mainstreaming used as lens causes any process, policy, or program to be viewed in a gender-sensitive manner. It raises two questions: What are the ramifications for men, and what are the ramifications for women? Are they equitable? For example, I often ask my classes, "What if a community decided to ban plastic water bottles? What are the effects for men, and what are the effects for women?" I ask the question in two parts, men and women separately, as means to get truly gender-sensitive answers. When the question is correctly phrased and answered, it raises awareness and causes gender sensitivity to be recognized. That recognition, in turn, becomes catalyst to ensuring parity.

The following types of questions can be asked:

- How does a new staffing schedule scheme affect the men in the organization, and how does it affect the women?

- When a proposed work-life program is suggested, did both men and women contribute equality, and are the effects on the male workforce and female workforce equitable?

- Does this new decision-making process allow for input from men and input from women in an equitable manner?

- Will this work group, this meeting, this panel have equal participation not only numerically but also and more so in terms of contribution?

- Does this proposed training benefit men and benefit women in equitable fashion?

Gender mainstreaming is the tool by which these gender-sensitive considerations are brought to light and inserted into the process. This is gender awareness at its finest.

With the principle of putting such focus on gender sensitivity, organizations should consider putting in place a gender custodian. This is a staff person who ensures gender is considered in various processes. This person might ensure gender and gender sensitivities are on meeting agendas, that gender is inserted into the discussion about implementing new programs, and that gender is an element in decision-making processes. They might also actively look through organizational policies and programs to ascertain gender sensitivity.

And finally, when it comes to awareness, don't discount the less formal, less structured, or even less educational-seeming activities and programs, such as walk in my shoes, job swapping, visits to other parts of an organization or to other teams, team activities, etc. All are means of raising awareness. For example, if one part of the organization is dominated by one gender, it would be beneficial, perhaps eye-opening, for others, especially others of different genders, to simply observe that unit.

All of these awareness efforts need to lead to a culture of awareness by everyone in the organization. Gender awareness creates gender-sensitive individuals, gender-sensitive leaders, gender-sensitive teams, and gender-sensitive organizations. When utilized fully and appropriately, an aware organization can avoid problems and, more importantly, realize the means to actually leverage gender and gender balance—men and women working together, respectfully, synergistically, and effectively.

Chapter 6

Safety

When a flower doesn't bloom, you fix the environment, not the flower!

Social Safety

In October 2018, women and men staged the Google Walkout for Real Change. Tens of thousands of Google employees from around the globe took part in a walkout organized in response to Google's perceived protection, and even rewarding, of men who sexually harassed their female co-workers. The organizers requested five changes:

1. An end to forced arbitration in cases of harassment and discrimination.
2. A commitment to end pay and opportunity inequity.
3. A publicly disclosed sexual harassment transparency report.
4. A clear, uniform, globally inclusive process for reporting sexual misconduct safely and anonymously.
5. Elevate the Chief Diversity Office to answer directly to the CEO and make recommendations to the board of directors. In addition, appoint an employee representative to the board.

The above were not difficult or complex requests. These requests could be in part solutions in many an office that, in addition to personal safety and comfort, could result in improved employee engagement, recruitment, and advancement.

In the case of Google, over the ensuing months the company committed to taking some actions. But that didn't stop shareholders from bringing a lawsuit against the board, claiming that it failed in its duties by allowing harassment to occur, approving big payouts, and keeping the details private.

Company leaders should take note: the desire for change is growing, and pressure is mounting from employees, customers, and shareholders to take an active stance to move beyond the status quo to create a business operating environment that is safe and equitable for all employees.

Early in 2019 a Gillette commercial called out "toxic masculinity." Despite threats of boycotts, Gillette shared its 48-second "We Believe" ad on its social media accounts. The ad played on the company's tagline of "Is this the best a man can get?" The intent was to address issues like bullying, sexual harassment, and the #MeToo movement. The result was both praise for and criticism of the razor company. "Is this the best a man can get? Is it?" a voiceover says in the ad. "We can't hide from it, it's been going on far too long. We can't laugh it off, making the same old excuses. But something finally changed. And there will be no going back. Because we…We believe in the best in men. To say the right thing. To act the right way. Some already are, in ways big and small. But some is not enough. Because the boys watching today will be the men of tomorrow."

When I was growing up, my childhood male friends and I were often admonished by our mothers and fathers that "boys don't hit girls." I can't say whether it was implied in that admonishment or not, but what really should be said is, "Boys, don't use your power to harm others—any others." There is a strong link between anti-bullying campaigns and pro-feminist campaigns because both are about treating others justly and fairly, and not using power to assail and belittle. That we have to tell and remind men not to engage in bullying behaviors more than we have to tell or remind women is telling itself. Those in power, typically men, need to be even more cognizant of power abuse. That is only a starting point. Men especially need to expand the message of "Do no harm" to "Ensure no harm." And in fairness, powerful women sometimes bully, too.

Google and Gillette are undeniably big-name organizations that have recognized security issues and the need to address them, despite potential ramifications. Sexual harassment and similar security scourges can no longer be simply text within policy; they need to be illuminated and actively addressed.

Sexual Harassment and Law

Sexual or gender harassment is verbal and nonverbal behaviors that convey hostility, objectification, exclusion, or second-class status about members of one gender. The legal definition of sexual harassment is "unwelcome sexual advances, requests for sexual favors, and other verbal or physical conduct of a sexual nature"—according to the Equal Employment Opportunity Commission.

Criteria for harassment (US civil rights law):

1. The unwanted behavior is severe and pervasive (enough to create a hostile work environment).

2. The behavior is perceived as offensive (regardless of intent).

3. A reasonable person must find the behavior offensive.

Experience tells us, however, that just quantifying something does not always qualify it in terms many of us recognize or relate to. Harassment is complex. A good many can't say they know when they see it, but at the same time too many can say they knew it when they've felt it. It comes in many shapes, sizes, and shades, and affects people throughout society and in the workplace.

- Sexual harassment statistics indicate 80–90% of women have been harassed in their lifetimes, and 38–64% have been harassed at work.[41]

- A 2018 survey by Stop Street Harassment found 81% of women have experienced some form of sexual harassment in their lifetime.[42]

- Male-dominated organizations are far more prone to sexual harassment. In fact, sexual harassment can be up to twice as common in male-dominated organizations as it is in female-dominated organizations.

- Troubling studies suggest that a number of men continue to hold on to vague notions of male superiority at alarmingly high rates. One study found that "only 17% of men wholly reject hostile sexism—implying that the vast majority of men cling to at least some sexist ideologies."[43]

An Equal Employment Opportunity Commission (EEOC) 2016 report[44] found, among other things, that:

- 45% of EEOC claims filed were sex-based.

- *At least* one in four women (25%) experiences sexual harassment in the workplace, and that number could be as high as 85%.

- 75% of harassment victims experienced retaliation when they reported it.

- Somewhere between 87 and 94% of employees experiencing harassment do not file a formal complaint.

- In the information, media, and telecommunications industries, 81% of employees reported experiencing sexual harassment in the last five years. An investigation by Victorian Trades Hall Council in 2016 found that 64% of women participants experienced sexual harassment or gendered violence in their workplace.[45]

Victims of Harassment

Violence against women has shown improvement in some areas. Hostile sexism (the misogynistic belief that women are inferior to men) is becoming much rarer. Attitudinal support for violence against women has declined. The majority of men are not openly, aggressively sexist, and broad trend data suggests that men's views of gender equality are improving. Attitudes toward gender equality have broadly improved.

And there is more to the story than what is prominently placed in the public eye. For one thing, sexual harassment is not exclusively perpetrated against women...

- In 2018 the *Washington Post* reported that nearly one in five, about 17%, of complaints filed with the US EEOC come from men, who are often targeted for not being masculine enough.[46]

- Up to 44% of men claim to have been harassed in their lifetimes.[47]

Then, too, there is the pervasive issue of harassment perpetuated against LGBTQ+ people. For example, a nationally representative sample of 489 lesbian, gay, bisexual, transgender, and queer adults found that more than half of them experienced slurs (57%) or offensive comments (53%). Most of those surveyed also reported that they or an LGBTQ friend or family member has been threatened or harassed (57%), sexually harassed (51%) or has experienced violence (51%) on the basis of their sexuality or gender identity.

Harassment against LGBTQ+ people is almost entirely sexual harassment as it is based on social sex/gender expectations. Though all groups are subject to such wrongfulness, gay men and transwomen bear the brunt of it. It is directly tied to the perceived affront of femininity and men. Lesbians are likewise harangued over perceived gender transgressions.

You can be a victim even if you are not a direct target of harassment. If minor occurrences are overlooked, they quickly become big ones, and they become part of the culture.

Regardless of who the victim is, sexual harassment always causes great personal harm. These harms are painful and can be devastating to an individual, and the effects can last a lifetime.

Workplace Harassment

Harassment is understood to be a societal and workplace issue as well, but those are not the common story lines.

While there is zero intent here to diminish the personal affronts and effects, we'll limit the discussion to safety as a workplace and gender balance issue.

A 2018 National Academies of Sciences, Engineering, and Medicine report unequivocally stated that sexual harassment is indeed more prevalent and more condoned in imbalanced workplaces.[48]

Harassment harms cannot be set aside in the workplace. By definition, a workplace is anywhere that business is conducted. This includes places away from the work facility itself (restaurants, conferences, outings, travel, etc.) where employees and staff my go or gather. Sexist attitudes and behaviors don't stop at the factory gate or office door, even those that lead to violence. In fact, the underlying drivers of violence against women can be traced to men's control of decision-making, limits to women's independence, stereotyped constructions of masculinity and femininity, disrespect toward women, and male peer relations that emphasize aggression. All of these are mirrored in our workplace structures and cultures, and all of these are facets of imbalance.

In the end, sexual harassment cannot exist unless the environment supports it. Organizational responsibility and consequences cannot be avoided.

Harassment Effects

The consequences for an organization that allows an environment where these things exist are matters of performance and legality. The latter hasn't been discussed much, but it can be truthfully said that an imbalanced organization is far more susceptible and liable from a legal standpoint. And the costs of lawsuits are astronomical. In 2015, the EEOC recovered $164.5 million for workers alleging harassment claims. Beyond that, employers face other direct and indirect costs in addition to legal fees. Hostile work environments lead to an unproductive workforce, increased turnover, and harm to the company's reputation. All of these take extensive time and money to repair. Some organizations never recover from the losses.

A 2017 Gender and Society study showed that "Eighty percent of the women in our sample who reported either unwanted touching or a combination of other forms of harassment changed jobs within two years. Among women who were not harassed, only about half changed jobs over the same period. In our statistical models, women who were harassed were 6.5 times more likely than those who were not to change jobs."[49]

As a performance issue, when a person is harassed or bullied, they won't feel included or empowered, and others won't see them that way. The reality is that a person in an unsafe or insecure situation will feel and be seen as disempowered and devalued. (Thirty-one percent of women have felt anxious or depressed at work because of harassment.)[50] These feelings manifest in behaviors. For example, women may disqualify themselves from certain assignments, isolate themselves for personal and/or emotional safety, or otherwise fail to follow through with top performance because they believe it is futile and causes unwanted attention.

Sexual harassment affects a business's bottom line in a number of insidious ways. Costs and performance are one thing, but the most egregious harm is employees not feeling safe. An organization that ignores, allows, or condones an unsafe environment is basically saying that it does not care about a group of employees, and that it is quite content to live with the imbalance of such and its consequences.

Lawsuits over sexual harassment and related issues or organizational problems are entirely avoidable. Despite this and all the harms of sexual harassment, studies show organizations typically respond to sexual harassment reports by inaction or minimizing. Where organizations do take action, those actions are far more often entirely defensive.

The law was relied upon exclusively in many workplaces for a great many years. But workplace laws designed to protect women are too often ineffective because they fail to address the overall gender inequality that women experience. Gender inequality experienced by women includes gender pay inequality, disadvantage and discrimination due to caring responsibilities, being subjected to gendered violence, and being undervalued in so many ways.

Safe Workspaces

To create safe workspaces, first it must be understood that sexual advances are much more often about power than about sex itself. Research attests men are more aggressive and have been more socialized to seek sex and believe they have a right to it as the dominant gender. Where men are in greater power, sexual harassment is more pervasive. More women in an organization equals less harassment. The more masculine an environment, the more likely sexual harassment occurs.

This may seem to be argument for balancing via numbers, and that is a solution, but why should it have to be, especially considering it is not an option for many organizations? Why not address what is a power issue with power solutions?

This power inequality undermines women's capacity to raise complaints, robbing them of agency and voice and creating insecurity. Without the capacity to raise complaints and pursue their rights, these rights remain unrealized. Therefore, any strategies designed to end sexual harassment and other forms of gendered violence at work must address the structures and cultures of inequality and sexism that exist.

Here is a to-do list to ensure a safe workplace:

- **Establish respect for all.** One means of getting the culture in the right direction is civility training. This has become quite popular as a tool to improve the environment, the culture, and working relationships.

- **Ensure the rules are clear, enforced, and effective.** That includes existing laws (federal and local) as well as local policies. Where the law falls short, create and adopt new policies and guidelines. Ensure all employees are aware of and understand the rules. Ensure zero tolerance of violation.

- **Have an open, safe, and fluid communications policy/plan,** one that encourages reporting. Ensure that there is an effective reporting system that is safe and easy to use.

- **Put response systems into place** that mandate investigation and satisfactory resolution to any aggrieved. Institute appropriate consequences for people who violate personal safety rules, including leaders who fail in their obligation to create and sustain a safe environment.

- **Train everyone** (and I do mean everyone) on how to spot, avoid, and respond to unsafe situations, including bullying, sexual harassment, and so on.

- **Equip bystanders.** Equip everyone with knowledge via training and also support, so that everyone knows they are able and responsible to intervene without negative ramifications.

- **Monitor and document.** Monitor the environment and employees. Document with the goal of capturing data that shows the true status of the environment and is transparent. Only a true picture will lead to appropriate solutions.

Bullying, Incivility, and More

With the intent of creating an environment where people feel safe not simply to work and contribute, but to contribute freely and fully, it should be realized that it is not just sexual harassment or bullying that limits a sense of security and hinders participation. Other shadows cast a real pall, including belittlement and disrespect, among other possibilities. Sometimes these things are seemingly insignificant manifestations that are misconstrued as innocuous. These may be comments, behaviors, or workplace practices that may be insensitive, discourteous, or inappropriate. They may have little recognition of such. But they are nonetheless contributing to discomfort among employers and an unsafe environment overall. You might even say disrespect is a gateway to harassment.

To reach the goal of creating a secure and embracing environment, business leaders and employees need tools for creating safe and respectful work environments.

Respect and similar issues can be addressed through civility training. Attendees of this type of training learn how to identify, prevent, and respond to any workplace incivility situations.

Employees should be also trained and coached on microinequities and microaggressions. Sometimes when microaggressions occur, the offending party is not fully or even partially aware of the offense. Often, microaggressions go unchecked because employees are afraid to voice their opinions, or they feel like they will suffer repercussions from speaking up or like they will not be taken seriously by the offending party or management. It's important for employees to know how to be handle microaggressions. And it's also important to teach and coach the harassed on how to advocate for themselves.

Unconscious and implicit bias training, as previously discussed, can also mitigate microaggressions in the workplace.

The way to truly reduce microaggressions is to have dialog. Having open and honest conversation about such targeted inappropriate behavior can reduce this type of behavior. This dialog can be handled safely in structured training events.

Bringing all of these things (incivility, disrespect, microaggressions, bullying, harassment, and so on) out in the open with dialog and training is important. Discussion identifies inappropriate behavior; otherwise the perception of inappropriateness is left as solely product of the eyes of the beholder.

Solutions: The Law
"When did giving a compliment become a crime?"

While it should not be so, sexual harassment still exists in shades of gray subject to perception. Too often behaviors go unchecked under the perception that the behaviors are simply not inappropriate. Too often, people are free to make these determinations by themselves. There may be little accountability where wrongness is so personally subjective.

Fortunately, harassment is not left to the perpetrator's interpretation. It is law—very distinct law, where harassment is clearly identified in objective form and the victim's perspective has more weight than the perpetrator's.

Law and supporting policies should be seen as objective tools of protection for all employees and staff. They are means of ensuring a safe environment. They should be neither feared nor abused.

Laws and regulations should not be viewed as defensive shields or swords to be brandished. I have seen agencies become so self-protective against laws being wielded against them that they use the same laws to hunker down and do nothing in the interest of assumed security. Certainly, laws and regulations can be foes as well as allies, but to see them in that light distracts from their worth as tools of change.

In addition to creating safe environments, laws like Title VII create value. They are tools of balance.

They may seem cumbersome tools, but by design, they do level playing fields and foster safety and inclusion.

Title VII is our cornerstone in the United States. I won't define Title VII here, nor will I debate pros or cons of that or any law. Different countries and governments have different laws and levels of protections. Regardless of where you live or whether you are an employee or management official, you need to understand basic employee rights under your country's laws. And if you conduct business internationally, you need to understand all applicable laws of where you do business. If you are not well versed in the employment laws in your country, I suggest you do some research. Employee labor laws lay the foundation for safety and inclusion. Not only do they define the field as it is, but they set the field for play. They represent the starting point from which all leveling activities spread.

In creating a foundation upon which an organization's safety culture is built, an architect (leader, manager, champion) must possess and fully understand the blueprints. The blueprints are the plan to build your safe and inclusive environment. And those blueprints must include applicable law at their foundation.

How thoroughly employees, managers, and organizational architects receive formal training in labor law topics varies widely. Typically, organizations do what I call "check box" training—training in which the overarching goal is to ensure that as many staff members as possible take the training and then check the box indicating completion. The focus is far more on efficiency than effectiveness. When efficiency takes precedence over effectiveness, organizations usually turn to mass delivery mechanisms. One of those is online training or webinars, which are minimally useful tools for awareness. This is like using labor law training as a defensive shield. It is more a tool of optics than a tool of change. To move past optics, the focus has to move to effectiveness rather than efficiency. Residence classes and other direct means may be more costly, but they can be much more effective. But they can be also be ineffective if they're not done properly.

Reporting and Other Supporting Mechanisms

An organization must not only train on law and policy, and do so properly; it must also put into place mechanisms whereby unsafe events are brought to light and ultimately appropriately acted upon.

A whole host of ills can be inoculated against if an organization has a good communications policy and supporting mechanisms. Openness and transparency are what allows problems to be brought to light and appropriately addressed. Without them, an organization is literally operating in the dark, with employees staying back in the shadows.

One communications mechanism that is a must in regard to safe environments is an effective reporting mechanism.

In far too many organizations sexual harassment goes largely unreported.

An Australian Human Rights Commission survey found that only 17% of those who had experienced sexual harassment made a formal complaint.[51]

Those experiencing it have little faith in their workplaces to deal with it. Many cited that they felt that a filed complaint would be seen as an overreaction, or that it would be easier for them if they just stayed quiet.

Reluctance to report is so strong that many harassed individuals prefer removing themselves from the situation rather than taking steps to ensure removal of harassment from the workplace. A 2017 survey of workers in the media and the arts found that people were generally reluctant to report harassment for fear of hurting their careers.[52] The VTHC study found 19% of women who had experienced harassment left a secure job because they didn't feel safe at work.[53]

And those witnessing harassment do little to stop it.

Almost 70% of those who have witnessed or who are aware of harassment did nothing to prevent it or to limit the harm that it caused.

This points to a culture in which gendered violence is normalized. It also underscores the broader gender inequality that exists in our workplaces and beyond.

Even where reporting itself is unhindered or not feared, there is still no guarantee of a safe environment unless those who cause insecurities face consequences.

Response tools must be put in place that:

1. Cause automatic and objective investigation.

2. Identifies and applies appropriate consequences where wrongdoing is found.

Fortunately, there are already very clear guidelines in these things as well as support from the EEOC. It simply takes leadership having the knowledge of these resources, the fortitude to use them in a consistent and objective way. Being inconsistent or playing favorites will do the exact opposite: make employees feel unsafe.

Vigilance and Monitoring

It might seem that if an organization simply applied the rules as given, the result would be a safe environment—one where women and men are free to fully contribute. The gotcha is making sure leadership's use of the rules is effective. The answer is to be cognizant and, more importantly, vigilant. Leadership must actively monitor the safety of their organization. Leadership must document personal safety items routinely and thoroughly, not only when events happen. Why?

Too many years ago to count I worked in IT; I did some network administration for a period of time and also taught classes in the same. I always told my students that they must monitor their systems always and not just when problems were noticed, because, as I told them, how can you identify abnormal if you don't know what normal is? Benchmarks are important. Really knowing how your environments, systems, and people operate on a daily basis is imperative to quickly noticing problems. Leaders can't be everywhere at all times, so documentation is a means of current awareness. Furthermore, documentation is a matter of historical measurement and awareness. Document, analyze, and repeat.

It should be obvious that much responsibility is laid at the feet of leadership—this is an unavoidable fact.

It is also true an organization's culture is a product of those in power. Again, in most organizations that is men. Men can be seen as both the problem and the solution. A great many men are trying hard to be that solution, and in doing so, they should not be penalized for good behavior.

Everyone should feel responsible for watching out for fellow employees with cognizance and standing up for them when they are wronged—especially for women who are harassed or anyone who is bullied.

It's not so hard to begin. Its largely about cognizance.

A study by Peter Glick and Susan T. Fiske (1996) revealed that men are less sensitive to and cognizant of subtle forms of sexism.[54]

The fact is that men are less likely than women to recognize both interpersonal and organizational forms of discrimination against women, and that they fail to recognize the severity of any form of harassment or sexism when it occurs.

To increase awareness, simply start by listening. Men especially need to listen to women. In listening, be there for your female colleagues. This is not the time to tell women in your field that not all men are violent or sexist. And if you want to be an ally, don't just express your sympathy; demonstrate your alliance by speaking out and supporting women. Recall that statistically, 70–90% of instances of sexual harassment go unreported. You may have to be the eyes, ears, and voice of organizational consciousness.

Self-education is also warranted. Know the bullying and sexual harassment laws and where to find resources for dealing with those issues. Educate yourself and share resources with victims. Identify sources of help aside from your human resources office. Educate others.

Zero Tolerance

Finally, in a safe and thriving culture, everyone practices zero tolerance at all times. Speak up when women are harassed or marginalized. When a male colleague makes a comment about a female colleague's appearance, contrast that immediately by saying what you appreciate about her work. When male peers make sexist comments, pull them aside and let them know how poorly their words and actions reflect on them and their institutions. Refuse to work with sexist colleagues. Make it clear to repeat offenders that they are harming everyone's ability to do their work. Don't invite them to events. Refuse to participate in events to which they've been invited, and tell the organizers why their participation makes you and your peers uncomfortable.

Inaction

These things don't sound so difficult, but they are difficult for a lot of people. Both men and women who don't want to get involved.

So why it is that men and women don't act? There are five main reasons:

1. **Non-awareness.** Obliviousness. A person may lack the knowledge of how to recognize inappropriate behaviors.

2. **Bystander effect.** The belief that others will take responsibility and act.

3. **Conformity.** Pressure/fear/trepidation at upsetting the opinion of the majority or acting against it. (Research suggests that men overestimate their peers' acceptance of sexism.)

4. **Psychological standing.** A sense of not having skin in the game, that the situation is irrelevant to them or that it's not their place to intercede.

5. **Fear.** Fear that they may lose something (and our primal brains prioritize fear and loss).

Of the five, the one that may get most attention is number 5. A form of loss is retaliation.

A 2003 study found that 75% of employees who spoke out against workplace mistreatment faced some form of retaliation.[55]

Fear may be a common reason people do not to get involved. But that same fear of retaliation may stifle admittance. This is commonly understood to be a big issue, so much so that there is actual law that offers some protection against retaliation.

Leadership can help. Leadership should help. One of the best ways to do so is to provide bystander training.

Obliviousness can be resolved through training, and so too can the other four reasons, through raising awareness and cognizance. Bystander training puts the focus on personal behaviors—the place where harassment occurs. It is actively proactive and actively reactive.

Forty-seven percent of employees said they know how to recognize gender bias, and yet only 30% actually addressed inappropriate language or behaviors when they occurred.

Bystander training teaches employees and staff how to prevent harassment, spot inappropriate behaviors, and address inappropriateness in real time. This type of training has proved more successful than the wrist-slapping approach of labor law and labor law training. In fact, this type of training was a major recommendation of the National Academies of Sciences, Engineering, and Medicine's report on sexual harassment in STEM (June 2018).

Can training help with understanding and installation of all these things, and truly assist in resolve such potent issues? The answer is yes—certainly when it comes to educating leaders, staff, and employees alike in what the rules are, how they will be enforced, and how everyone will play their part. Beyond that, training can get to behaviors and behavioral responsibility.

Still, even the best training has its limits in terms of what can be imparted that will stick.

Training needs to include and be followed up with activities that engage all. These could be role-playing exercises, case studies, panel

Q&A, or other activities that include dialog. Dialog fleshes out the nuances and impacts of the issues rather than exclusively focusing on rules and procedures. Creating ongoing, subsequent activities is even better. For example, having employees engage in the subject in areas of the organization other than their own work area.

In the end, companies that implement these types of training events enjoy fewer harassment- and discrimination-related complaints, investigations, and legal troubles.

Only when the whole of the culture changes is an environment safe.

Anything short of that should be seen as condonement of harassment and bullying, and in turn is condonement of lack of full participation by all—lack of real inclusion.

Change is slow, but the data tell us that overall we are making progress, at least in some places.

Chapter 7

Inclusion

Diversity and Inclusion Shortcomings

Inclusion is often a misunderstood concept. I believe a huge part of that is that diversity and inclusion are (too) commonly tied together as in D&I (diversity & inclusion) or, more recently, DEI (diversity, engagement, and inclusion) programs. Typically, the D garners more attention than the I, with the focus put on the makeup of an organization. Thus, solutions are focused on recruiting and creating a diverse workforce. There is nothing wrong with diverse recruiting efforts of course—unless it removes attention from ensuring an inclusive environment.

Another issue is that far too many D&I programs are wholly centered on diversity awareness activities rather than on actions that leverage a diverse workforce in the interest of inclusion. Too many D&I programs gloss over the indispensable inclusion side of the coin.

Work-Life Programs as Inclusion Tools

A huge part of inclusion is being accommodating to employees as much as is feasible. If we truly aspire to ensure everyone is indeed included, we must ensure that work systems embrace the worker and ensure that are no hindrances to a person being able to contribute. This is not lost in appropriate D&I programs where inclusion is addressed through programmatic solutions. One thing many organizations have gotten correct more recently is instilling work-life programs. And while these are not necessarily seen as D&I, they are very helpful in regard to inclusion.

Work-life programs are a huge leveler. Work-life programs address both numbers-bound and non-numbers-bound solutions. Of the former, the programs are an essential recruiting and balancing tool, as will be discussed later. These programs work on a number of balancing levels. For one, they make a person feel more comfortable, something especially important in imbalanced organizations. Comfort means performance. Consider how flex hours, telework/telecommute programs, or on-site childcare can affect how well a caregiver can focus on work once these needs have been addressed. In a workplace with no such programs, employees can waste much of the working day worrying about childcare arrangements, for example. In an imbalanced workplace, time and energy are also lost to thoughts of guilt, defense of necessary personal activities, and the like.

According to the US Equal Employment Opportunity Commission, a major challenge hindering advancement is the lack of flexibility for women raising young children. The report says agencies should expand job-sharing and telework policies, offer different start and end times for workers, and create satellite work centers to reduce commutes.

It seems to be a simple issue: the more that can be done in accommodation of workers' needs, such as child-rearing, the more they can be engaged in the workforce. If nothing else, it is a huge matter of retention.

Simply give women, and men, more choices in this. But there is more to the story.

Consider this: according to new data from a recent Deloitte survey (as reported in the *Wall Street Journal*, June 2019), while more companies are beginning to offer new fathers paternity leave, many working dads aren't taking it. The survey found that "a third of male participants feared they would be putting their careers at risk if they took days off to care for their newborn. More than half of the participants admitted that taking parental leave would send the message that they are not committed to their jobs."

This is not simply a matter of accommodation. Nor is not a just domestic issue. Rather, it is organizational balance issue. It is not just a matter of absence we are talking about, but more one of power that directly impacts the ability of workers to contribute and influence, and also a perception of commitment, among other things. The stigmatizing needs to end. Programs need to balanced not only for accommodation but also for standing.

While the benefits of work-life programs are becoming better and better known, implementation varies depending on perceived costs. In fact, costs are not a factor, because there are actually cost benefits to the programs.

In some organizations, reluctance to put work-life programs in place is simple stubbornness—a reluctance to change. It might be assumed that the issue is male stubbornness at putting in place things that seemingly may be of more benefit to women. But you might be surprised by a recent study that found that female-dominated workplaces have fewer and less flexible gender-sensitive programs than do male-dominated workplaces. This may be a matter of women leaders believing they are doing right by the women in their organization simply by being there. Presence in numbers, however, does not equal real representation or allow active presence.

Work-life programs have proven themselves to be agents of inclusion.

To be effective, these policies and programs need to appropriately include gender sensitivities (and be fully supported by leadership).

Gender needs to be a consideration in design and implementation. A gender-sensitive lens is used to view and understand how policies and programs affect people of all genders, regardless of the gender makeup of the organization.

Consider, for example, family-friendly policies, which are largely based on female caregiver and male work-dedicated models. But are they truly equal to both genders? The androcentric workplace that still dominates today tends to perpetuate man-favoring policies and practices. Many of these institutions reward work accomplished as the result of long work hours, for example. Such a philosophy hinders women who often can't work long hours because of childcare responsibilities and other societal expectations.

Organizations need to put gender-sensitive work-life programs in place and make them work. Policy solutions can also address gender balance by addressing gender-insensitive situations and evolving cultures. All of this requires concerted, long-term effort. Otherwise, these cultures and their practices stubbornly persist.

A number of organizations are looking at programs that assist in accommodation. Whether or not that is seen as directly addressing inclusion or as only a response to demand is debatable. Too often inclusion is left just hanging out there somewhere.

Inclusion and Presence

Then, too, where inclusion is a worked-toward goal, it is often misinterpreted as exclusively to make a person feel welcome and a part of the team, group, organization, or institution and to acknowledge a person's right to presence. Again, these are not bad things. In fact, they are necessary. We want everyone to feel welcome and comfortable, and we want everyone invited in. The nuance is with the word *presence*. Presence can be seen as a person simply being and hopefully feeling comfortable, part of a group. The problem is that of passive versus active. It is not enough that a person is present in body if that person is unable to fully participate.

A 2018 Pew Research Center study using data from the Bureau of Labor Statistics looked at image searches of 105 occupations.[56] In more than half of occupation searches, women were underrepresented relative to the number of women who actually do those jobs. That means, for example, that although women make up 23% of announcers, they were only 12% of people pictured as announcers.

If women aren't represented appropriately in imaging, how well are they represented in voice?

Inclusion means not only being present but having presence. It means being given a seat at the table *and* being allowed to contribute and influence in parity with others.

Typically, this is a matter of women being given voice. In male-dominated workplaces, it's not about the number of women in the building or even seated at the table (though that is a step toward inclusion); it is rather that women are given opportunities to speak and contribute in balanced fashion.

In the true-life story portrayed in the movie *Hidden Figures*, three African American women known as "human computers" worked for

NASA at the time when the United States raced against Russia to put a man in space. In preparing to launch astronaut John Glenn into orbit, one of these women, a tremendous mathematician named Katherine Johnson, is assigned to the Flight Research Division. Johnson was given the assignment based on her knowledge of analytic geometry and overall ability with numbers. Before her arrival, the division was entirely staffed by white men. In the beginning, her assignment was very much undervalued, and her work was questioned or ignored. Additionally, Johnson wasn't given the information and support needed to successfully do her job—information was actually hidden from her. And, as was sadly too common in those times, as an African American woman she was the subject of obvious discrimination in a number of forms. Johnson had to endure significant discomfort and fight hard to contribute and prove herself. In the end, however, as history attests, she became invaluable to the space program and, in the process, garnered some of the respect she so deserved.

In the case of Katherine Johnson, we see that it is not nearly good enough to diversify in concept but not in practice. It was not enough, not anywhere close to enough, to simply allow her into the group. It is not enough to invite people into the room but not give them a seat at the table in the form of voice. Katherine had to fight for her voice. It was the fight that allowed her to contribute in the grand and superior way she did. The group benefited from her talents because it allowed her voice.

As it was then so, too, is it now. As it was/is at NASA so too was/is it everywhere. It is not enough simply to add a woman to reap benefits of diversity. For Katherine Johnson to contribute and make the positive impact that she did, it took a systemic change. One of those changes was giving her the data she needed despite previous protocol, and then valuing what she did with that data. Still she had to prove her work's worth and her personal worth time and time again.

It should be noted that Johnson's finding her voice took someone championing her cause. That, too, is part of systematic balancing (and will be discussed later). In her story we also see a dynamic: the aforementioned phenomenon of prove it again. This phenomenon is one that women uniquely face in the workplace. They are required to prove themselves—repeatedly, as Johnson did.

It is worth noting that in 1962, the year of John Glenn's launch, the advantages of diversity were unrecognized; in fact, they were not even considered. Thus, the intent of bringing Johnson into the work group was not simply to diversify; the Flight Research Division simply wanted another mathematician, and she was near at hand. But rather than recognize the mathematician, they saw an African American women, gave her work, and expected no contribution based on her gender and skin color alone.

Even today, where an organization might consider that diversification is a good thing in and of itself, too many of organizational leaders believe the diversity benefit is about optics. They believe they should diversify only because a sector of society suggests that diversity is a good thing somehow, and they wish to be seen as a diverse organization.

Women are still too often added to the boardroom to be seen and not heard, to be tokens of representation. Some organizations believe that simply having a woman or a number of women present adds something somehow, without really knowing what that something is. Sometimes that something is believed to be a perception of credibility.

Some organizations believe they are more credible if they merely appear to include more women.

Luckily, many are becoming aware of this shortsightedness…but not all.

In another true-life movie—*Zero Dark Thirty*—we see examples of when optics are assumed to be enough in lieu of actual contribution. In the film, and in real life, the character Maya is the CIA analyst whose dedicated and superior work post-9/11 was directly responsible for finding Osama bin Laden. More than once, the film portrays Maya being called into high-level US security meetings only to be told to sit aside and be quiet, even though she knew more about the subject at hand than any other official in the room.

In one poignant scene, the CIA director calls a meeting with high-level intelligence advisers to try to determine how accurate their intel is. Maya's presence is requested. One adviser, Dan, says there's a 60% chance there's a high-level target in the suspected house, but he doesn't know if it's bin Laden. Another adviser, George, says 80%. But another adviser, Jeremy, asks Maya what she thinks. Given the opportunity to have a voice in this room of men, Maya says confidently, "100%." Maya was given space, and she put herself forth confidently in that space. While her forwardness raised eyebrows with at least some of the men, the CIA director was impressed with her answer despite her demeanor being out of line with her position (and what's considered typical for her gender).

The CIA director's positive impression of Maya was not a full embrace of her contribution, however. As the group leaves the room, the director says to one adviser, Jeremy, concerning the others, "They're all cowed." Jeremy says that Maya is "fucking smart," and the director replies, "We're all fucking smart."

Even when women have a voice, there is no guarantee it will be valued. In fact, study after study attests that far more often than not a women's voice is given less credibility than that of any man who may be present.

Even when women have a seat at the table and a voice, they still must deal with the issue of credibility. And too often credibility is in the hands of men in power. It can be said that men control credibility. They get it, have it, and give it. One study found that women in science who have male spouses also in science are published 40% more often than unmarried women or women with spouses in nonscientific fields.

Credibility issues are but one source of silencing voice and diminishing female contribution and influence.

Imbalanced representation itself is a hindrance to voice. For example, a Freedom of Information Act request to the Engineering and Physical Sciences Research Council by the *Guardian* revealed that from 2007–2008 to 2015–2016, women were underrepresented on peer review panels that determine who gets a grant and how much, taking fewer than one in five of the seats. As recently as 2013–2014, women were outnumbered nine to one in panel meetings, and though the figures have improved, today women still make up fewer than a third of review panel members. The impacts illuminated were that in 2016–2017, fewer than 7% of all research grants went to teams led by women—the lowest proportion for 10 years. Additional data shows 90% of engineering and physical sciences funding in UK goes to male-led projects. Even when women successfully apply for funding, they are awarded less money than their male colleagues. The average size of grants to women was less than 40% of what their male counterparts received.

To ensure active presence, inclusion policies and programs have to be created and implemented to that end. We noted earlier that some countries have laws that mandate levels of gender balance in executive boardrooms. Some large international organizations have gender mandates in place for all policy and program meetings. Mandates for greater presence-prominent balance can be placed in many organizational processes—for example, goals for the division of work on committees.

Putting policies, guidelines, and other practices in place that make space is just a step in allowing real presence.

Organizations need to get the underrepresented in the room, at the table, and contributing.

Once those people are present, procedures can be put in place to give them equitable voice in a great many activities. In meetings, committees, presentations, publishing, and so on, rules and procedures can be established to enable more balanced contributions. Roles can be created to enable greater involvement in the processes. The more structured the process, the more equity is instilled. The less structured, the more bias and power holds sway, usually at the cost of female contribution.

Where Are the Women? Increasing Participation

To reach parity of presence, organizations might also need initiatives that identify women (and underrepresented men) who can be added to the processes as contributors. Initiatives can identify when and how they might do so. Registries of female speakers can be created. One example of this is Request a Woman Scientist, which connects an extensive multidisciplinary network of vetted women in science with anyone who needs to consult a scientist for a news story, invite a keynote speaker or panelist for a conference or workshop, or find a woman scientist to collaborate on a project or serve as a subject-matter expert. In addition to registries of people who can be tapped in the interest of parity, registries of events that represent opportunities for voice can, and should, also be created.

To increase participation, attention must be drawn to the issue of participation.

Just because an agency is imbalanced in male/female staff does not mean it should be imbalanced in participation.

Cognizant observation is needed to ensure participation, inclusion, and balance.

Such cognizance needs to become habit as part of that workplace culture. Each event should be seen as part of the whole, part of enduring organizational culture. And it should not be acceptable to make exceptions in the interest of convenience. It may, for example, seem prudent if pressed for time to include only those readily available at the cost of balance. In a male-dominated environment, that will always mean men are more conveniently included. Convenience, of course, is no excuse for exception and rarely leads to the best outcomes. Too often imbalance goes unquestioned and unabated.

It is entirely possible—and depending on the makeup of a group or organization, it might even be probable—that an all-male (or all-female) configuration is wholly appropriate given need, availability, experience, and so on. Any number of variables and reasons may legitimately cause any occurrence to be so imbalanced. But that should never be assumed to be the case. The question of appropriate balance and representation is always a valid one.

Until everyone asks why there are few women at the table, there will continue to be few women at the table.

Without cognizance, change won't happen, and without questioning, cognizance won't happen. The questioning often takes the form of "Where are the women?" If a panel or meeting or work team is all men, or even a clear majority of men, the question is, "Where are the women?"

In working with a large federal agency in the not so distant past, I witnessed an example of calling out disparity. This agency supported several Facebook pages for various groups of employees. A post to one of these pages showed a group of men testing new software during a testbed exercise. A female ally called out the post and noted that no women were involved. I was also a member of that Facebook group and asked, "Where are the women?" The post got a lot of attention, and people commented that it was either wrong or no big deal. I knew the manager of the testbed and chatted with him. He was initially defensive, but he explained that the men invited into the simulation were indeed experienced and experts, and thus, it was appropriate. But I pressed further and asked if that meant there were no qualified women. Of course, there were, but the men involved were there as matter of the norm from previous simulations. I was finally able to get him to see that even if there are reasons a group is so constituted, that does not make it inappropriate to ask, "Where are the women?"

Status quo remains status quo when it is unquestioned and unchallenged.

The vast majority of time, conference panels and boards are filled with a disproportionate number of men, and thus greater male voice. Most keynote speakers are men. High-profile articles are frequently written without female contributions. News stories are reported by men far more often than by women. And men are quoted within articles and news stories far more often as well. All these and other similar forms of imbalance amplify male voices and minimize female voices—minimize contribution and influence.

"Where are the women?" Ask the question.

Beyond that simple question, I recommend that more powerful, more affective behaviors should also be undertaken. If you see, for example, a panel with no women, ask the question and recommend qualified women. When you organize panels, meetings and such, target gender balance and ensure diversity. If nothing else, refuse to participate in non-inclusive events and activities.

Aside from formalized settings such as meetings or conferences, there are other areas in which procedures or registries can increase presence and be applied in everyday tasking to create space and opportunity for inclusion. For example, pre-leadership stretch jobs or details can be created. Registries of qualified women or underrepresented men can be created to fill those roles. Rotational assignments or walk-in-my-shoes programs can provide exposure and experience as well as tie directly to contribution and influence. Research clearly shows that one way to close the gender gap is to make sure all staff members have a shot at high-promotability tasks. Not only is the gap closed, but balance is fostered. Furthermore, by inserting underrepresented women or men into new roles, the organization grows that person and their abilities. This is a function of personal development, a concept many leaders believe in strongly even when they may not believe in inclusiveness. Stretch jobs and details should not be such a hard sell.

Work Structures

To be more inclusive, managers should exercise some flexibility in how work itself is structured and tasked. For example, as noted previously, men are more often socialized to be more competitive with others than are women. To make the most of this difference, organizations should organize work around such preferences.

Work evaluations can also foster inclusion. Again, in understanding male and female preferences, for example, if the job is sales, some salespeople may be ranked against other salespeople, while some salespeople may be ranked against some benchmark or quota. The decision is based upon the individual person's traits and preferences, the accommodation of which encourages maximum contribution.

Leveraging Strengths and Authenticity

One sticking point is that some people, including managers, see preference as only a matter of personal choice, and personal choice should be set aside in deference to environmental conformity. However, it should be understood that one's preferences most likely represents one's personal strengths, which ought to be accommodated and leveraged as much as the environment allows.

In leveraging preferences, which very often do represent one's greatest strengths, self-evaluation of those preferences is a mandatory step. Tools such as the MBTI (commonly known as Myers-Briggs), DiSC, StrengthsFinder, and so on can yield valuable information about people and their preferences, strengths, and so on.

Once properly assessed, everyone in an organization should discuss their strengths with those they work with and for. Implementing a rule of engagement for appreciating others' strengths and ability to contribute levels the playing field. It allows for both the celebration and execution of real diversity.

In the end, not only should individuals be conscious of preferences and strengths, but so should organizations.

To maximize contribution, it is incumbent upon an organization to have an understanding of the preferences and strengths of all leaders, staff, employees, and workers.

This requires of an organization supporting the use of analysis tools in the workplace, such as MBTI, DiSC, StrengthsFinder training, and so on.

As it relates to preferences, this seems a good place to revisit the concept of authenticity.

Individual authenticity is important for organizations as well as individuals. This is where inclusion comes in. After all, being inclusive means being inclusive of each person and what they have to give. People who are authentic bring their whole selves to their jobs and participate fully and honestly in the workplace. Organizations that place a premium on conformity at the expense of authenticity may be incurring hidden costs. Organizations that are selective instead of inclusive incur the same.

Real inclusion does not enforce conformity; rather it allows all individuals to bring all of themselves to the table, to be unique individuals.

In the days following 9/11, former New York City mayor Rudy Giuliani was asked about his leadership during the calamity and what leader he admired. Giuliani answered, "Winston Churchill." He went on to express his admiration of how Churchill handled the events of World War II. Next, Giuliani was asked how he tried to emulate Churchill. He responded emphatically, "I wouldn't do that. Why would I do that? I am not Churchill. I have to do what I do best."

No one can truly be successful in trying to emulate someone else. Nor would anyone dispute the value of authenticity. In fact, authenticity is the superior leadership style de jour. However, taken to the extreme, authenticity can be faulted. Too often it becomes a source of obstinance, when what it should be is as a means of personal consistency and transparency.

My favorite story on the topic of authenticity is a piece I read about Mohandas Gandhi. After Ghandi gave a lengthy speech in London, a reporter asked one of Gandhi's assistants how Gandhi could speak so long without notes. The answer: "What was heard was Gandhi. What Gandhi says is who Gandhi is. And who Gandhi is is what is being said."

Speaking from the heart about things near to your heart, or speaking about things not only known but understood and lived, fits my definition of authenticity. Being one's self.

But being and doing may at times be different.

Where authenticity is most powerful is in coupling personal authenticity with flexible and adaptable leadership behaviors.

There is strong evidence that when it comes to leadership, the most flexible people do best. Take the concept of situational leadership, for example. This highly successful practice of using the correct leadership behaviors appropriate to the situation has stood the test of time as practice of a great many successful leaders. Consider also why diversity itself is heralded—because with diversity we are able to tap into diverse skill sets. It is the ability to flex many options that one is best able to adopt and address any circumstance accordingly.

As an irrefutably authentic person, Gandhi was at the same time quite flexible to situation. He is known, of course, for passive methodologies, but that was not his only methodology. He was direct at times and strategic at others. He couldn't have been successful in any of his endeavors if he had not been adaptable.

Authenticity should be desired, while at the time expansion of one's authentic skill set should be encouraged…and fully embraced.

Authenticity is not an excuse to take a "my way or the highway" position and stubbornly sit pat, avoiding learning and using new skills.

Authenticity has value in representing all of your traits and strengths—those you've held for many years and those newly acquired.

Women and Balancing Authenticity

For women in today's workplace there are a lot of pressures to be this or that, including to be authentic. At the same time, women are still advised to "be one of the guys" or "lead like the men do." But there are real problems with the efforts of balancing being authentic while trying to be more conforming of masculine leadership expectations. At times it takes constant consideration of the proper lane and associated adjustments, oftentimes recreating themselves. Because they do not fit the masculine stereotype of leadership, women create a persona that gives them credibility and authority without forgoing their sense of self.

Instead of all this searching and trying to be like anyone or anything else, learn what works for you. And then learn other things that can also work for you. Your personal brand of innate authenticity should be one means to bringing your unique behaviors, skills, talents, strengths, and traits to the table as a woman *in addition to* other behaviors, skills, talents, strengths, and traits that can and should be acquired. Wield them in a flexible manner. Authenticity is a starting point—not an end.

Women are burdened by constant balancing. It may seem unjust, because it is not a requirement for men in most places. It would be easier to either stick stubbornly with being authentic or conform to the environment, often a masculine/androcentric one. There are costs to either bad choice. If a woman chooses exclusive authenticity, she will miss the opportunity to learn valuable new traits that are workplace necessities. And if a woman chooses conformity, she pays a high personal price in subjugation of self. In a vain attempt to live up to organizational norms and expectations, a woman's behaviors may go against her own values. And it's not easy being a phony. It takes a lot of energy to behave in ways that are out of sync with true values, priorities, hopes, characteristics, and style. The energy expended trying to come across as something one is not is energy unavailable for work performance.

On a recent podcast I was asked the question "What one thing do you know?" My answer was that everyone has closets. And while the term *closet* or *closeted* is associated with LGBTQ+ people, I submit that we all have part of us we keep in reserve, pieces hidden to ourselves. No one gives or shows all of who they are or what they have to give. This reserve is very valuable. The more of ourselves that we put forward, the more we have to give in contribution. This ties back to safety and ties into inclusion. An organization that fails to tap into all a person has to give, sets itself up for much greater failure.

In concluding this chapter, I hope I have made one thing clear: inclusion does not mean assimilation. Throughout this chapter the balance between inclusion and assimilation (e.g. conformity) has been highlighted. While it's not generally an issue for men, women feel these balance issues very keenly, and especially so in imbalanced workplaces. When the balance issues are most pronounced, many women see the matter as a personal choice to sell out or get out. Among other things, this directly affects retention and perpetuates organizational imbalance. On the recruiting side of the coin, organizational balance is likewise negatively and perpetually impacted by unsettled choices for women. On a job application in a male-dominated field, does a woman play up her feminine strengths, such as being supportive or a good listener, or emphasize traits more associated with men, such as assertiveness? Resumes of women are disadvantaged by the double bind as much as women's behaviors are.

In the end, the more flexible one is, the more one is able to not only contribute but succeed—assuming, of course, the environment is inclusive in embracing all a person has to give.

In the next chapter we'll further explore inclusion of everything a person has to give—specifically inclusion and utilization of gendered traits.

Chapter 8

Inclusion of Gendered Traits

If one of the principal goals of gender balance is to ensure maximum contribution by all genders, then valuing and utilizing everything a person brings to the table is a requirement.

There is no shortage of evidence that an organization is most successful when it appropriately leverages many traits and attributes. In fact, most will recognize that truly valuing what a person has to offer and embracing that fully—meaning allowing full exhibition and utilization of one's traits—is inclusion (and the opposite is exclusion).

Undervaluing Valuable Traits

Inclusive trait utilization issues are worsened the more imbalanced and organization is. Because power remains on the side of men in most places, feminine traits are devalued and subjugated to male leadership traits. And where men are in power they are free of the requisite to change the skill set that has seemingly served them well.

Yet, the fact is that both sexes have strong valuable trait sets. Unfortunately, too many feminine traits are devalued and discouraged as workplace behaviors.

If you want proof of traits being devalued, just look at how they are appraised.

Many beneficial traits that women use frequently are seldom found in evaluation criteria. Feminine skills such as empathy, sensitivity, caution, language skills, and relational abilities are especially absent. While it may be more common these days to see words such as *collaboration*, *cooperation*, and *coordination* in job announcements, position descriptions, and evaluations, those behaviors are much less rewarded than are, say, individual command, project leadership, and other masculine traits. The big-picture effects are seen in studies that continue to conclude that people as a whole see men as better at management because of their evidenced, or assumed, masculine traits.

So, how can an organization achieve parity in contribution and influence when a whole bunch of valuable skills and behaviors are not given value, not allowed to be included in work processes?

Let's look at a couple of examples of underutilized gendered traits.

There are many examples of devalued traits, skills, and behaviors that have profound impacts on performance and, in turn, direct impacts on organizational success. But trust is a good example to start with. Trust is an important thing for an organization to have in abundance. It is the foundation of all relationships and personal interactions. In the workplace, it has a big impact on both relationships and performance—they are inextricable from one another. Despite the well-known value of trust itself, the elemental behaviors required to build trust are themselves not always valued.

Before we get to trust behaviors, I will point out that we humans trust people who are like us and distrust people who are different from us. Men may more readily trust other men, and women may more readily trust other women. Of course, that is not always the case, and there are many factors that affect this. One factor is the amount of gender balance. The more imbalanced an organization is, the less one sex will trust the other.

What serves an organization best in creating a culture of trust is inclusive use of trust-building behaviors by men and women.

According to a field study of trust conducted by military psychologist Patrick J. Sweeney, there are three central factors in trust building: competence, character, and caring.[57]

We'll start with competence. People are more trusting of competent people, so behaviors that demonstrate competence can be an easy way to build trust. In fact, I like to tell my classes that competence is the easiest way to build trust. "Simply do your job and do it well." Yet, if you recall our earlier discussion of prove it again, women have to work harder than men to get the same credit for the same work—2.5 times harder. Women have a harder go at building trust with others in this way. Devaluing the contributions of women in the organization means women may be unjustly less trusted. That most certainly has a negative impact on teamwork and the organization.

We'll leave character out of the discussion because, frankly, it means too many things to too many people. That said, I will point out that a number of character behaviors can be seen and categorized as masculine or feminine traits. These again should warrant embracement regardless of which gender may exhibit them more often.

The other trust-building trait is caring. Caring is extremely important to organization. And yet, as a feminine skill, caring is far undervalued, especially in comparison to many other leadership traits that are much more highly prized and fostered. In addition to the many other benefits of caring as a trait, it can be the quickest way to build trust—if it is valued.

Let's look at one other trait or skill as an example of the importance of balance in gender traits, one that was touched on briefly in the last chapter: flexibility. To keep the discussion from becoming unwieldy, I will limit it to how it relates to leadership styles.

Flexibility and Masculine and Feminine Leadership

I've chosen leadership because it is also a matter of empowerment. Of course, either sex can benefit from flexible leadership skills, but as a matter of leveling the playing field, it can be argued that women need this more. When I conduct women's leadership workshops, flexible leadership is a major piece of the training. It is an immensely important topic for women, and also for men.

In varying situations, men and women may take different approaches and use different strengths (traits). However, it has been found that overall men and women lead very much the same. I will add a caveat to these statements by noting that the research is inconclusive. But this is not surprising when you consider all the factors, which include social pressures, workplace conformity, stereotype effects, education (including informal self-edification), biology, and so on.

So, is there such thing as a feminine leadership, for example? Of course there is. If traits can be categorized as masculine and feminine, and a person tends to use traits predominantly from one trait category or the other, then, yes, you could have feminine leadership. And you could have masculine leadership. A person who uses a more democratic leadership style could be said to be doing feminine leadership. And a person using a more autocratic leadership style could be said to be doing masculine leadership. Recall that it is more appropriate to assign a gender (masculine or feminine) to traits than it is to assign traits to gender (sex). Thus, a gendered leadership style is not, nor should it be, tied to one sex or another. A woman might practice masculine leadership and a man might practice feminine leadership. However, the question that many people are really asking is, "Is there female leadership versus male leadership?" Even though more women do practice feminine leadership, the answer is an absolute no. Leadership style is gendered but not sex bound.

The feminine traits commonly found in women cannot help but find their way into the ways in which women lead. In general women have a more democratic leadership style; they are better social leaders. Women tend to prefer consensus building over conflict and are good mentors, coaches, and team builders, among other things. Studies have found that women actually outscore men in most management categories. One study showed women fared better in 28 of 30 leadership competencies, including problem-solving, planning, controlling, managing relations, leading, and communicating. Likewise, women exceeded men in 15 of the "Top 16 Competencies Leaders Exemplify Most."[58]

Furthermore, women in general are more people-centric then men, who are more thing-centric. It can also be said that more women are transformational leaders versus men who tend to be transactional leaders. As feminine and transformational leaders, women in general can be adept at working in partnerships. Women take care of others in taking care of the organization. In fact, 33% of employees are engaged when a women runs the show, compared with 25% with a man at the helm.[59] And in the same study, women were found to be better at encouraging their subordinates' development and checking in on their employees' progress, and they tended to provide more positive and constructive feedback.

Likewise, the masculine traits found in men and discussed previously cannot help but find their way into the ways in which men lead. In general, men use a more autocratic leadership style. They tend to be dominant leaders with strict expectations; they give orders and take progress reports. They ensure systems, processes, and employees are working efficiently. In this way, men are more commonly transactional leaders. They take charge and are more likely to emerge as group leaders and task leaders.

This may seem a contradiction to my earlier statement that men and women lead very much the same way, but again, the research is inconclusive. Keep in mind the situational and motivational aspects of traits. Furthermore, the use of traits is often a matter of exception and subtlety. While general statements can be made about masculine versus feminine, transactional versus transformational, and democratic versus autocratic styles, there are actually an infinite number of ways a leader can lead, because any one person is made up of any combination of traits in varying amounts. Each trait can be plotted anywhere along a spectrum representing the level of that trait in terms of masculinity or femininity.

Both feminine and masculine leadership styles are essential to guide an organization to success. Transactional leaders provide distinct advantages through their abilities to address small operational details quickly. Transactional leaders handle all the details that come together to build a strong reputation in the marketplace, while keeping employees productive on the front line. Transformational leaders are crucial to the strategic development of the business. Businesses with transformational leaders at the helm shoot for ambitious goals, and they can achieve rapid success through the vision and team-building skills of the leader. Both styles can be leveraged only where both styles are present and valued.

A number of institutions (educational, consulting, and so on) developed (and in some cases, marketed) what is called situational leadership. Among these is Ken Blanchard Companies. In Blanchard's work, leadership varies in the amount of directive behaviors and supportive behaviors. These could also be called masculine behaviors or feminine behaviors or transactional behaviors and transformational behaviors. In any case, the former could be said to be very direct and specific—what, when, and how—and involves activities such as organizing, educating, structuring, and focusing. The latter involves behaviors that encourage, foster, involve, and empower. Direction is replaced with listening, collaboration, and delegation. Blanchard actually identifies four distinct leadership styles: directing, coaching, supporting, and delegating. These span a behavioral spectrum from very hands-on to very hands-off.

The fruitful work by Ken Blanchard Companies further identifies when and how these various behaviors should be applied situationally. Situation is determined by an employee's or a team's development stage. This approach is not unique to Ken Blanchard and Companies. In fact, earlier work by psychologist Bruce Tuckman used the now well-known team development stage labels of forming, storming, norming, and conforming. The concept succeeds only when a person's situationally chosen leadership style is correctly matched to an employee's (or team's) overall development stage.

Regardless of origin or packaging, misuse of the approach results in either over-direction/over-supervision or over-delegation/under-supervision. The former is more (in)famous and is commonly referred to as micromanaging.

With situational leadership there is no wrong leadership style. Rather, there is only wrong leadership style application. That's also true of all masculine and feminine leadership styles and behaviors. It's not that one gendered set or the other is better; rather, it's a matter of fully leveraging diverse styles. This necessary diversity of leadership styles is more prevalent in gender-balanced organizations.

As we have discussed, men are better versed in masculine leadership styles and women are better versed in in the feminine style. *Versed* means practiced. But more important than the ownership and practice of this style or that style is the ability to be flexible in using multiple leadership styles. *Flexible* is the key word.

The appropriate behaviors are applied in flexible fashion, and yet flexibility as a trait is not universal. Many people struggle with flexibility. We all have penchants and habits in the ways we like to lead. The source of these can be, and often is, gender, which is largely wrought through socialization. Lest you believe something like flexibility is not a socially constructed trait, consider this. Research found that the less time children spent with their parents, the more gender-flexible the children became. Flexibility itself is a malleable trait.

Previously we discussed the difficulties women have in trying to conform in male-dominated institutions, be authentic with themselves, and balance masculine and feminine behaviors. According to a study in *Psychology of Women Quarterly*, showcasing manliness is a better career strategy for women.[60] Women who described themselves with traits traditionally associated with men (independent, focused on achievement, etc.) were seen as a better fit for the job than those who emphasized traits often seen as more feminine (warmth, supportiveness and nurturing). A 2011 study in the *Journal of Occupational and Organizational Psychology* found that women who are aggressive, assertive, and confident and who can turn those traits on and off depending on the situation get more promotions than either men or other women.[61] Again, what is being advocated is situational fluidity.

But authenticity cannot be disregarded. In this, many women are told, or assume, that to be authentic they must staunchly stick to and lead from who they are and not even consider accommodation. Women in my workshops have cited their authenticity with a variety of comments: "Why should I have to conform?" "Why should I change?" They are actually saying, "I'm really good at doing things this way. Why should I have to do it that way?" Why change? Because it may be requisite to success.

For the record, I'm not going to tell anyone to conform. However, while it is true that a person, any person, should lead with her or his personal strengths, that is not an excuse to turn one's back on acquiring and using new strengths. Stubbornness is the enemy of flexibility. And from an organizational perspective, the more diversity of skills present, the more success can be had. This is the true value of diversity and inclusion.

Ideally, men and women would be able to flex a full suite of behaviors, be they masculine or feminine.

Flexibility functions very much like being multilingual. Some call this ability being gender bilingual or being gender agile.

Women have been much better at this then men, primarily out of necessity. Women have learned to be flexible as a result of male power as well as influence to be more accommodating in general. Overall, women are, and have been, quicker at gaining cross-gender skills. In recent studies, women increasingly describe themselves with more typically identified male traits such as aggressive or risk-taker.

Men are less flexible because flexibility is a trait less practiced by men. Men are more rigid when it comes to the way they operate in the workplace. As the dominant gender in most institutions, as well as the socially empowered sex, men have been largely inattentive to any adaptation and avoid learning cross-gendered skills, because they haven't seen a need. Yet, while it may seem of more importance to women, men too would do better being more agile.

Let's continue looking at leadership traits that are given disparate consideration or value.

To begin, we often think that leadership is largely directing, moving pieces to produce things for others. But better organizations understand that good leadership also involves caring about their people. To be effective, employees need, among other things, to be respected, valued, and cared for. In fact, many companies are very good at treating employees like family.

As one case in point, Starbucks has as much of a reputation for how it treats its workers as a reputation for coffee. Since 1992, Starbucks has been rated one of the best companies to work for. It is known for "nurturing and inspiring the human spirit." You might ask, "What do nurturing and inspiring have to do with being a strong leader in a competitive world?" In truth, nurturing and inspiring have everything to do with leadership. The real problem is that nurturing and inspiring are not comfortable ways for a lot of men to lead. Women leaders, however, are more acquainted with thinking in familial terms. Connecting with people can be considered a more feminine skill. Women are often more "take care" than "take charge" and more transformational than transactional.

Many men still need to learn how to show they care and need to learn to lead with heart. I say "learn" because we are talking about a gender skill. And as a skill, it takes practice—investing time in relationships at work, getting to know employees and stakeholders as if long-lost family, and being both an example of and a catalyst for camaraderie, caring, growth, and empowerment. To succeed, male leaders need to be willing to augment their likely masculine approaches of leading with feminine approaches, and the organization needs to encourage them.

Leaders have to be able to be transformational and take care of people. At other times, they need to take charge and be transactional. Leaders need the right tool for the right job, and they need to be able to pull that from a toolkit that includes both masculine and feminine tools.

The Value of Multiple/Mixed Traits

The value of a trait is far more important than whether the trait is possessed by a man or a woman.

Because value is situational, the more traits that are present among employees and leaders, the more likely it is that the company will have the right trait on hand when needed.

An organization can have a better suite of traits when the organization is properly balanced. And that includes both a balance of men and women, and a balance of traits among men and women.

On an individual level, either sex can benefit from using a mix of masculine and feminine traits. As was the case for women and masculine skills, studies have proven that men who have strong feminine traits actually excel more than men who only possess and exercise strong masculine traits.

Particular challenges have made men slower to adopt cross-gender skills.

As a group, men are simply more rigid and unyielding. While this could be simple stubbornness or ego, there are extenuating factors.

Men traditionally don't seek help, for instance. It's a male taboo that is societally enforced in most places and in many organizations. Even when men do reach out for assistance, there are fewer support systems in place for them. As an example, while men may enjoy some great advantages such as sponsors (discussed in a later chapter), they are missing out on other resources. For one, the number of and current push for structured empowerment programs are largely directed toward women. There is appropriate rationale for this, but there is also cost to men who are left out. This then being a case of non-inclusiveness that disfavors men.

Then too, in similar fashion as women, men have had a hard time escaping their traditional roles. Men also are boxed in by gender expectations. Men are expected to be dominant, assertive, decisive, ambitious, competitive, aggressive, in control, independent, bold, strong, tough, responsible, confident, and direct. And while men are also encouraged to be funny and easygoing, they are not encouraged to show emotion. Sure, many books and scholars suggest it is good for men to get in touch with their emotions, but in the real world, men who too closely heed such advice are called wimps, pansies, or any number of mocking labels. Men who exhibit traits that are not "manly" are often outright ostracized by other men.

As a result, men have a harder time acquiring a feminine skill set to augment traits that have previously served them well. The truth is that many men will feel some level of disconcertment just reading some of the things here about feminine skills. The binary gender system can be blamed for the prevention of acquisition of feminine cross-gender skills by men, but it cannot be used as an excuse. If we want a workplace where both men and women can utilize both masculine and feminine traits to their own and their organization's advantage, we need to remove all sex discriminatory beliefs and behaviors.

The issue with reluctance toward gender agility on behalf of men may seem to be a harm unto men themselves—and yes, it is. And it should also be seen as a harm to organizations, as it is. But is this a harm to women? As long as men hesitate to change, and as long as their trait set and associated behaviors remain those that are sanctioned, non-inclusiveness toward feminine contributions will continue.

Real inclusion means actively embracing all gender attributes and fearing none.

Men and women must both be willing to exhibit and use masculine and feminine traits appropriately against even against our own comfort zone, and even where the environment itself may be discouraging of such use by one gender or another.

Cross-Gender Skills Training

Once we clear the mental hurdles, both the devaluation of some traits/skills and reluctance to acquire others not already in our tool kits, we can focus on cross-gender skills acquisition. How does one acquire any trait, regardless of gender classification? Again, traits are behavioral skills and, like most skills, can be learned. How does one learn empathy, for example? As with everything, learning empathy begins with the elementary. In the case of empathy, we start with self-awareness and build from that. Many women are given such lessons as little girls. They are asked what they are feeling and then asked to consider what another may be feeling. Such behaviors are exercised and practiced until empathy becomes a skill. In the workplace, empathy can be built into assignments and tasking as well as into training and workshops.

Training, such as cross-skills training, is certainly a big piece of the balance puzzle that is an organizational responsibility. Leadership should:

- Conduct gender training that is intentional and focused as opposed to tiptoeing around, disguising, or slipping in with other trainings. Training needs to be specific to the fact that a specific gender skill can and should be used to achieve such and such. Don't minimize gender skills by relegating the discussion to a few topics such as personal communications. Nor should gender be limited to diversity training. Rather, in more broad fashion, find a place for the subject in many more business/job trainings.

- Eliminate the term *soft skills*. *People skills* is a start, but it is disguised and generally not focused enough. Call it leadership, team-building, or communications training if that is more appropriate. But if the training is gender-focused, say it is.

- Delve into the causes of sexism and the devaluation of certain traits. An understanding of the social and patriarchal impacts can be valuable. Most certainly, there should be a component addressing bias, especially unconscious bias.

- Don't segregate your training. I know many argue that empowerment training should be for women only, and I have led that type of training many times, but I feel strongly that men and women need to be put in the same classroom and work the exercises together, especially role playing and case studies.

- Approach gender-skills training through contrast and comparison of differing styles, approaches, and methods. Case studies work especially well for this.

- Train people in the use of the correct traits in the right situation. Thus, when it comes to this key training, situational (gendered) skills use also needs to be taught.

Once we embrace and become inclusive of the whole spectrum of gendered traits and skills, we are free to be fluid in their use. Such flexibility propels one person, group, or organization past others with less fluidity. In the interest of maximizing contributions and subsequent success, it's up to organizations to encourage this. Organizations must openly encourage fluidity the same way they encourage anything—by supporting and rewarding it. Organizational leadership must ensure the environment fosters a culture of gender fluidity that maximizes contributions in all gendered forms.

Chapter 9

Allies

We have all had someone in our lives who has lifted us. It may not have been professionally, but we understand that aid from trusted others can help us be better. And *better* increases our value to others in return.

Allies are one of the five fingers that organization can use to tip the scales. This chapter is all about those others who help.

An ally is a person or group aligned with and supportive of your beliefs and goals, most often in the professional arena. *Alignment* is not passive, however; it should mean support of those goals in active fashion. Real allies don't sit idly by sharing your positions. Rather, they stand up for you in actions and behaviors. Using geopolitical allies as analogy, allied countries don't stop at simply seeing things the same way as their aligned countries. They follow that up with supportive actions that range from vocal support to monetary support to battling common enemies. At an organizational level and personal level, the same should be expected.

These days, initiatives such as HeForShe are helping raise awareness that men, too, have a part to play in gender equality. Feminism is not just for women, nor is feminism only about women. The word *gender* means all genders. When it comes to gender balance, many of the balancing programs and initiatives have direct and positive impact on men as well. Allies can be of any gender for these same reasons.

Male Allies

I had a surprising conversation with a fellow gender balance consultant—a very successful and well-known consultant, I might add.

During a conversation on gender balance, she stated that "women don't need men." This of course raised my eyebrows.

In most workplaces, women come in second place in a two-person race. It is especially important that men be involved in solutions even if they don't readily see these as male issues. It's not that women can only achieve because men support them, but is it is helpful to have supportive, influential, and caring allies, a number of whom are men.

The fact is that the involvement of men is necessary in many organizations in order for equality, parity, and balance to take hold.

Again, this is largely due to the fact that men hold the power in most organizations. They hold the keys to the castle.

According to United Nations Secretary-General António Guterres, "Our world needs more women leaders and more men standing up for gender equality. It is true I am a man, but we need all men to stand up for women's empowerment."

I had an interesting discussion with a group of international male hydrologists about gender equality, of all things—yes, male scientists talking gender as the topic of choice. The discussion took place in Rome after I had completed conducting a women's leadership workshop for female professionals in hydrology as a part of an international hydrology conference. I was at a reception atop the City Museum of Rome and found myself at a table with about eight male hydrologists and one female hydrologist. Needless to say, I was surprised at the topic of conversation, because I expected to discuss something scientific. But this group of largely older white men launched into a lengthy discussion exclusively about women's empowerment, gender equality, and feminism. To a man, each recognized many of the issues women face and wanted to help. It got very personal. I tell this story often as testament to the willingness of men to entertain such a conversation and their willingness to be allies. You can call these wonderful, brilliant gentlemen scientists or feminists, but here we will call them allies.

A large percentage of men want to stand up. Between 20 and 40% of men want to support women more in the workplace.

However, many may be ill-equipped to do so.

The National Science Foundation finds that male allies need to do three things to create institutional change to support gender diversity.

- They must share the insider knowledge of the organization they have.
- They need to show genuine understanding of the cost of inequality for everyone as well as for the organization.
- They need to demonstrate honest commitment to what is right and just.

Empathy and Vulnerability

In addition to the three actions above, I want to add two more actions that I believe to be essential in helping women. The fourth action is empathy.

We have to acknowledge the importance of empathy in supporting anyone who is undervalued, set upon, or the target of any of the negative behaviors discussed earlier in this book.

It has been found that empathy is often realized by men by having other women close to them in their lives. In fact, men with daughters have been found to be more cognizant of and empathetic to female concerns in general, as well as to overall female inequality.

The fifth action is credited to my fellow author, consultant, and colleague Julie Kratz. In Julie's book *Male Allies*, she states that "to be truly supportive of women men need to be vulnerable."

Empathy and vulnerability are inextricably linked.

In order to be truly empathic, a person has to open up to others. They have to drop their own defensive thinking and in so doing become vulnerable. This vulnerability enables openness to other's experiences and in turn may lay vulnerable one's own perspectives.

Another aspect of vulnerability that I will note here is being subject to pushback. Pushback on your support of others can come from many different directions. You may be set upon by folks who strongly disagree with your supporting position of the undervalued for any number of reasons. As one example, there may be men who see you as a traitor, possibly taking away from them and giving to women. You may be set upon by women who believe you are playing favorites. And you may even get pushback from those you are trying to support. Your support may be seen as disingenuous or misplaced. In putting yourself out there, you have to accept that you may become a target.

Cognizance vs. Action

It should be seen that being an ally is a matter of all of cognizance, emotional commitment, and supportive activity. The emotional piece takes on many forms—vulnerability (as described above), ownership, and empathy, to name but a few. On the latter, I know many men who truly try to understand the concerns of women and make real effort to empathize with and support women. I also know women who support other women. Empathy and emotional support are huge pluses to others; standing by and saying "I feel for my female colleagues" is not enough. Allies must do more. Having difficult conversations is laudable. But again, more can be done. The greatest support comes from the activity.

In an upcoming book (yet to be titled) David G. Smith, associate professor of sociology in the National Security Affairs department at the US Naval War College, and W. Brad Johnson, professor of psychology in the Department of Leadership, Ethics, and Law at the US Naval Academy, assert that allyship encompasses both interpersonal skills—listening, empathizing, and engaging in reciprocal, collegial relationships—and taking a public stance in the workplace, calling out sexist behavior, sexist comments, or salary discrepancies that harm women,

Johnson states, "It's not enough [for a male ally] to be kind and competent interpersonally. Women also need public allyship. It's being the guy who calls things out when something is unjust, including sexist behavior and comments from other men. If the man who's an ally sees discriminatory policies that put women behind or make it tougher for them to step away from family obligations, he steps up to remedy that."

I recall a CEW study that indicated men's "engagement" is not necessarily translating into enough action, or at least the kinds of action that will make a difference. As I recall, the study found that most men in the workplace (76%) are supporters of gender equality and can see that gender equality benefits their female friends and relatives. Seventy percent indicated that they sit somewhere in the middle—they are neither highly engaged nor fully disengaged. Only 17% of men, however, are "highly engaged" and "prioritizing action." And more than half of men, 55%, ranked gender equality as a "low priority" or "non-priority."

Just as importantly, the report found that perceptions about men's engagement differ significantly between men and women. While 64%

of male respondents feel satisfied with their current level of engagement, women tend to disagree.

Almost 70% of women said that they would like men to be more involved.

This is a huge gap in perceptions of a critical workplace issue.

In the end, while the numbers show the need for support, it seems that too few are prepared to do anything meaningful about it, or perhaps they just don't see what they might do to actively support women.

I might suggest that many men incorrectly believe that to take action as an ally involves becoming a full-blown feminist and fixing gender inequality the world over. They may balk as to the perceived scope. But the reality is that there are many things a male ally can do that are easily within their capabilities.

A big thing male allies can do is show self-restraint, step aside, and simply get out of the way. Men can be cognizant of the space they take up in conversations, at meeting tables, at conferences, at the lectern, and on panels.

I have often seen speaker panels at conferences void, or nearly void, of female panelists. Even when female panelists are included, they are far too often talked over by male panelists. I've even seen that happen at diversity and female-empowerment conferences. What I said about inclusion previously in regard to women's presence holds true. When you see an imbalanced meeting, panel, class, or slate of speakers, a supportive action as an ally is to ask, "Where are the women?" When there is no appropriate rationale for the lack of women participants, decline to participate yourself. Allies can make a huge difference by bringing more women to the table (meeting invites, panel invites, etc.). I advise the same when there are meetings, panels, and so on that are all women. Ask, "Where are the men?" Or invite them in. I also advise this of men for events of female empowerment or other women's conferences and events. Men need to be part of the solution, so they need to be part of the conversation.

It doesn't take much to call attention to exclusion, devaluation, disempowerment, or other wrongs. Speaking up and extending invitations along with any of the other items above are small actions to take to rectify biased unfairness. Too often, we settle for thinking right instead of doing right.

Here are some things that a gender ally can do, male or female:

- **Recognize your unconscious biases.** Recognition is the first key to bringing about change. Take time to identify what your biases are and where they might play a part in your workday. Then make a plan to address them and consciously follow through with actions of mitigation. This applies to both men and women. If you recall from chapter 2, studies find that both men and women have gender biases.
- **Do your homework.** Seek to understand the needs of both male and female employees, and strive to provide what is needed. Don't make assumptions, and don't defer the responsibility to educate you to the women you work with. Seek out women's perspectives, recommendations, and opinions. Ask women to share their stories. Open your door, and then open up the conversation.
- **Look for ways to make room for women's voices.** Ask women to share their stories.
- **Share emotional labor.** Don't rely on the women in your office to provide all the emotional support.
- **Take time to identify where women might play a part—or a bigger part—in your workday.**
- **Respect women's boundaries.**
- **Commit to intolerance of discriminatory and harassing behavior**, especially sexual harassment, which is most often perpetrated against women. When you see such behavior, call it out for what it is: wrong.
- **Be a vocal advocate.**
- **Be a nudger.** Encourage women to speak up and participate.
- **Make it known and obvious that you are an ally.** Champion and encourage others to be the same. Be an example.

While the items above can be best practices of any ally, male or female, I will reiterate that it is especially important for men to do these things. Men have more power to bring about change as power-positioned allies. I caution men, however, that having and wielding power to help women does not make you a hero. It means you are simply doing the right thing in being a gender ally.

Many men don't understand they have privilege that gives them power. They may just lack a realization that they do have power to do something. This is especially true as men were socialized to be fixers, and if they can't see a way to solve something (such as gender equality), they may feel powerless. Here are some ways that women can nudge men:

- Ask them to attend a women's employee resource group event.
- Ask to have lunch together to collaborate on a particular challenge you are experiencing.
- Ask for an introduction to another colleague you want to work with in the future.
- Ask them to put your name into consideration for a big assignment or promotion.
- Ask them to help get you involved in being a part of a diverse interview slate for the hiring team.

Female Allies

With all the talk of male allies, both here in this book and in the public sphere, you might think that female allies are a nonissue. You may believe they are a given. One might believe that women are more naturally allies to other women. But what often occurs in imbalanced work places is tug-of-war.

As a strategy in male-dominated workplaces, women often pit themselves against each other instead of helping each other.

Women can and do bully each other. Furthermore, if the only way to get ahead is to separate yourself from other women, some marginalized women are going to do just that. Some women may get along better with men because it pays to get along with whoever is at the top. Women simply don't have the same status in American life that men do. When people ask themselves, "Who do I want to work with?," they subconsciously leap to the default: the historically revered man.

There are other theories about why a woman may go after another. There's favoritism threat or women's concern they'll seem biased if they help other women. There's competitive threat when a woman fears a female newcomer will outshine her. Then there is system justification, which is a psychological concept in which long-oppressed groups, struggling to make sense of an unfair world, internalize negative stereotypes.

Surveys by the Pew Research Center and Gallup Poll as well as several academic studies show that when women have a preference about the gender of their bosses and colleagues, that preference is largely for men. A 2009 study published in the journal *Gender in Management* found, for example, that although women believe other women make good managers, "the female workers did not actually want to work for them."[62] The longer a woman had been in the workforce, the less likely she was to want a female boss. Interestingly, study participants were biased against women only when they were asked about the gender they preferred to work for in general. When participants were asked about their current bosses, the bias disappeared. It could thus be seen that gender consideration is a primer for gender bias, which indicates that in imbalanced environments where gender is more on people's minds, biases are stronger.

Whatever the reasons, women don't always get along well with other women in the workplace. A number of experts agree that this discord between women in the workplace is sometimes nothing short of cattiness. It can be about hidden agendas, grudges, passive-aggressive behavior, or judging. Whereas interaction between women can be "catty" at times, it has been found that workplace discussions between men and women are typically all business, about the work and getting it done.

None of this suggests women would be better off allying with men. Women can be one another's best allies when they can see clear benefits. There are many benefits, and there are many examples in which women have been invaluable to the success of other women. One way women can work together was clearly evidenced in the Obama White House. In meetings women used amplification strategy. When one woman spoke in a meeting, other women repeated what she said. They echoed each other's ideas and credited the women who came up with them. They vocally celebrated one another's achievements. This forced men to acknowledge the women had just as much to contribute as the men did.

Amplification represents women empowering other women as allies of and for each other. If you are a woman, I hope you feel a responsibility to help other women. Work together for success instead of engaging in any form of tug-of-war. It doesn't take large measures to support rather than antagonize female co-workers. In order for women to be allies, they need only help in small ways to ensure women are valued and not devalued, seen as friends instead of foes.

Gender Champions

Next up, I want to switch to another, very powerful, type of ally: gender champions. And to introduce gender champions, I'll switch from movie examples to one from literature. (Okay, I'm cheating. This example is both a movie and a book). Consider Fanny Price in *Mansfield Park*. In taking a position at Mansfield Park, Fanny was given the position of house servant despite her connection to the family. But Sir Thomas Bertram, the head of the household, would not allow Fanny to remain in such an undervalued position; rather, he included and promoted Fanny. His intervention was more than anything a matter of being a vocal ally. It would be a stretch to call him a gender-equality champion, but he acted the part by calling attention to inequities within the household.

In the workplace, gender champions do just that. They raise awareness of disparities and champion the cause.

Champions assist in gender parity on a broad scale more so than as aid to an individual, as would be the case with a sponsor (discussed in a later chapter). Because of this, champions do not necessarily have to be in positions of influence, although that is helpful to the cause. This means any of us, in positions of influence or not, can be gender champions. To be a gender champion, we take on the role of active and vocal allies—allies who support and foster our disadvantaged female (or possibly minority male) work colleagues. In the bigger picture, gender champions espouse the principles of gender balance, parity, and equality toward a more embracing and effective workplace.

At the organizational level, many organizations do encourage gender champions and male allies. Some formal programs are very well known—for example, the United Nations program HeForShe. But while many understand the intent of the program, the how remains unclear to most. As with allies, the question for gender champion is "What do I do?" Even where programs, such as HeForShe, put out a ton of good information that illuminates the issues, their effectiveness is limited because the how-to is often absent. It is of little use if champions are only tokenistic, limited to wearing a ribbon, for example.

As an instructor, I couple instruction of concept with practice. I suggest the following examples of what can be done to go beyond the desire to be a gender champion and move into action. I have found it useful to frame the statements as pledges.

- I pledge to make known to all staff that I am a gender champion and that my door is open to all to discuss any gender issues in the workplace. I can also provide resources concerning gender issues or otherwise direct anyone to such resources.
- I pledge to read at least one recently authored book or report on gender equality and share a review of it with those at my workplace.
- I pledge to review and understand the organization's guidelines and policies related to gender as well as pertinent equal employment opportunity laws.
- I pledge to commit to including gender topics on at least 50% of meeting agendas.
- I pledge to conduct or participate in gender-awareness campaigns and activities.
- I pledge to equitably increase opportunities for empowerment of both genders in terms of training, assignments, job shadowing, and so on.
- I pledge to thoroughly explore the UN HeForShe website or similar resources of gender equality.
- I pledge to be a supportive co-worker or manager and be an ear to listen and a voice to call out inappropriateness.

- I pledge to recruit others as gender champions.

These are just a handful of examples of what a gender champion might commit to. A number of organizations I've worked with have used such pledges as a way to formalize a gender champions program or awareness campaign. Anyone in an organization can make such an honest and committed pledge.

While position is not a requisite to being a gender champion, leaders are, nonetheless, in a position to be even more powerful champions through broadened efforts such as the following:

- **Recognize your unconscious biases.** Because recognition is the first key to making a change, take time to identify both what your biases are and where they might play a part in your workday, whether recruiting, rewarding, workplace relationships, or other areas. Then make a plan to address them. For example, you may find that you unconsciously favor men for certain tasks, in which case you make an effort to find ways to assign such tasks to women more often.

- **Focus on recruitment, hiring, and promotions.** If you are responsible for hiring or promoting, embrace the notion that a diverse workforce is essential for optimum performance. It is both a matter of practices and mindset, and recruiting efforts can easily be targeted toward underrepresented groups, such as women. Tipping the numbers is a direct path to balance. If you are not directly involved in these efforts, you can still encourage them, or at least offer input.

- **Bring women into the decision process.** Women are often absent when their careers are being discussed. Too often the discussion of a women's career involves only men.

- **Invest in female employees.** Take the time to identify programs or initiatives you can join or create to support the growth of employees. Make the programs and initiatives known to all, especially to female employees. Give women seats at the table. Build stretch jobs. Understand what barriers have a gender bias and remove them from women's paths to leadership. Focus on and intervene in the early steps to women's leadership. Get women into roles that provide access to senior leaders who can serve as advocates for women's careers. Share tangible, constructive feedback with women. Provide role models.

- **Create a safe, inclusive environment.** Have zero tolerance for any forms of non-inclusion, disempowerment, devaluation, disrespect, discrimination, harassment. Take immediate action if such occurs. Ensure everyone knows all resources for official redress.
- **Ensure others know the issues and benefits of an inclusive, balanced workplace.** Explain to and educate others about the importance of proper treatment of all and the benefits of gender balance. Provide training.
- **Be visibly transparent.** Make known the issues in tangible ways. For example, have someone keep track of who does the talking in meetings ("time of possession") along gender lines. You may be surprised at how imbalanced this. Make known salary levels. There are many things that can simply be given the light of day.

This is a brief listing. There are innumerable ways to champion the cause. The important thing is that the ways are active and visible, so they not only help people who are disadvantaged and undervalued, but they also help create more allies and champions.

Ally Groups

Allies come in many forms. They don't have to be individuals.

Most large organizations have in place employee resource groups (ERGs, or sometimes called affinity groups). Employee resource groups are voluntary, employee-led groups that focus on shared identities/affinities and experiences and look to apply those perspectives to initiatives that create value—value being the great leveler toward balance.

For organizations, ERGs enable attraction and retention of diverse talent, provide employee development opportunities, educate on issues and programs, and foster employee engagement (among other things).

For an individual, they offer support, assistance, and resources.

And isn't that what allies are all about? Where organizations host ERGs, there is typically one for women. As with individual allies of women, ERGs support the cause of women in the ways identified above.

I have a lot of experience with employee resource groups, having formed and led many, including women's groups. So, of course, I have a list of best practices, but that list is short—just two items:

1. **Have a passionate champion and a passionate grassroots membership.** Ensure that an influential leader is steeped in the activities of the group. The involvement of a person in position of power will empower the group as a whole. However, the influential leader does not necessarily have to lead the group itself—in fact, it is better if they do not. The best ERGs are grassroots efforts that allow for input, influence, and effect by a number of people throughout an organization. This ensures appropriateness of activities.

2. **Separate the ERG from controlling entities.** The ERG should not be under the direction of HR, diversity and inclusion, or any other entity that will direct its activity. Just as with a grassroots membership, the idea is to be very open to allow grassroots and other solutions to arrive from many different directions and in many different forms.

Two items seems like a very short list. But truly that is all that is needed.

A strong champion in a position of power gives such a group credibility in the eyes of everyone up and down the organization. Plus, the champion is in a position to resource the group as needed. Credibility and resourcing will sustain the ERG and its ability to actually do things. Without such support, a group will be ineffective or in time wither and die.

The grassroots membership adds to credibility as well. But of even greater benefit it that is from the grassroots that appropriateness is instilled—appropriate ideas, appropriate programs, and so on—items that truly meet the needs and accommodate those the ERG is meant to support. If we're being honest, organizational leadership does not know how to meet the needs of all in the organization.

Also note the criterion of passion. That should go without saying.

Those involved must passionately believe in what they are doing. It is a necessity for momentum. Without it, it is really just a support group in name alone.

Finally, a truly supportive group must have autonomy. Control chokes off the innovation and flexibility that is needed to find new ways to deal with very old problems. Autonomy gives the group the freedom to be adaptive and inventive.

I was once charged to head a gender focus working group to find ways to empower and support the needs of women. We were extremely effective in the beginning, because at first we were able to fly under the radar. Once our work gained good notoriety, a leadership official wanted a piece of it and pulled the group into his existing office structure and direction. We were subsequently choked to ineffectiveness. If ERGs are going to be allies, they need to be set up to serve their constituents' needs more so than organizational wants.

Another form allies can take is that of structured circles, which also function as networking groups and are recognized as a key ingredient to female success. Circles are small groups of people who meet regularly to support each other and learn new skills together. Members talk openly about their challenges and ambitions. Circles function logistically differently from networks but overlap in terms of what is discussed and what the benefits include. Even though circles are a relatively recent concept, it has been found that women in such circles are more aware of the role gender plays in the workplace, and they are more likely to ask for—and receive—raises and promotions. Circles are support mechanisms, problem-solving mechanisms, and, most importantly in terms of organization balance, value enhancers. Circles are another way to build relationships and share data, and they can be another means for individuals to build social capital that can yield huge dividends.

Research has found "that while both men and women benefit from having a network of well-connected peers across different groups, women who also have an inner circle of close female contacts are more likely to land executive positions with greater authority and higher pay, while there was no link found for the success of men in terms of the gender composition of their inner circles."[63]

As suggested above, circles are not just for women. Research has shown that people are more confident and able to learn and accomplish more in small groups. While circles are more commonly targeted at women, they can be of benefit to men also.

To get the most out of a circle, the recommendation is to limit the size to eight to 12 members who are at similar stages in their careers or at least have the same workplace issues and aspirations. While it is best for people in circles to meet in person, if that is not a workable option, there are alternatives. Circles can be virtual. They don't necessarily have to be live in real time, although greater benefit can be derived in being so. A number of social media platforms can fulfill some circle functionality. I have seen a number of organizations use Facebook pages or Google hangouts to great effect and benefit. I have often been surprised at the level of participation, the breadth of topics tackled, and the depth of ideas shared—all very openly—in these forums. I have seen circles work as a catalyst to additional work-life programs, employee support and empowerment initiatives, and other balancing initiatives. Circles are effective in a number of forms and are relatively easy for organizations to implement. If the organization won't organize circles, employees can do it themselves.

Networking as an Organizational Function

When it comes to allies, I want to include a pitch for networking as an organizational responsibility. Typically, networking is seen as an individual effort—a means of individual self-empowerment. It is, and it will be discussed in that realm in full in a later chapter in that context.

Networking facilitates meeting new people who may assist in one's cause. Networking creates opportunities to building relationships that create trusting partnerships, make you better known, put you in good light, and enable more opportunities to contribute and influence. It is important enough that it should warrant organizational attention.

According to a study done in 2016 by Mc. Kinsey & Co. and LeanIn. org, men often have more opportunities to spend time with senior executives or work on the most important projects or even meet the most valuable clients.[64]

Over the years, this leads to increased exposure for men at the workplace, thus creating a higher probability for them to be promoted or sent abroad for an assignment as compared to a woman who's been working alongside him.

Here again is evidence that women are not getting the same contribution and influence opportunities that would be beneficial to all. But imagine a company, agency, or institution creating and maintaining a networking database. Imagine a list of people who could act as introductory networking agents for new-hire employees during onboarding. Or imagine a list of mid-career networking agents that could be presented to mid-level professionals and career-enhancing networking agents who could help those looking to move up. And imagine if there were folks called networking ambassadors or networking liaisons whose job it is to help employees network within the organization. Making networking information available creates a cadre of agents of balance and performance. It seems to be a relatively simple way to increase value, at least no more daunting an endeavor than current, common mentoring programs.

Then, too, companies could have less formalized processes that allow all employees, irrespective of gender or years of experience, to meet and gain knowledge and exposure from their seniors. Getting-to-know-you sessions, randomized group meetings to discuss careers, and so on—any such format can go a long way in inculcating an atmosphere of equality.

Networking is a means of empowerment and balance. It adds value (weight) to individuals, and it tips the scales as part of the ally finger.

Allies come in many forms, but regardless of form, they can function as value raisers. Organizations must recognize their importance and not only encourage workplace allies but support them in tangible ways. Leadership should see their role as ally providers.

Chapter 10

Authority

The fifth of the five means to manually adjust the gender balance scale is authority. Authority is the enforcer. In the scale analogy, it could be seen as the thumb, as it carries (the most) weight.

Note that I use the word *authority* as opposed to leadership, as authority can take more than one form. Typically, authority will come from organizational leadership. Authority in that form can be seen as the easiest to put in place and likely the most powerful. But authority can also be granted to, or arise from, other powerful entities. Empowered and self-empowered groups or individuals can and do carry authority as well. They can be very influential people in an organization who are not positionally empowered. Or they can be groups that have influence, as matter of self-achieved credibility or having been anointed with it. The latter is granted power by another authority. The test of what constitutes real authority is if employees, staff, and stakeholders see it as such.

All leveling activities carry far more weight when they're backed by authority—again, typically that is upper leadership. That likely sounds obvious, but it is not obvious to all. Sometimes authority is assumed when it is not present. Sometimes leadership may address imbalance through optics alone, or it may abdicate responsibility altogether. Perceived authority is not always effective authority. What is needed to adjust the scales is real authority that can exercise power or at least give credibility.

Recall that the other four fingers that can modify the scales are awareness, safety, inclusion, and allies. Authority must not only be present alongside the other four; it must actively operate as catalyst to the other four. It must give them life and make them living agents of balance rather than inert ideas living only on paper and in word. Where any of the other four may falter at times, authority must carry the weight—that weight being responsibility and ownership—and put its thumb on the scale as needed.

It may sound heavy-handed, but the analogy here does serve a purpose. There will be times when balance must be addressed by decree of a person or group of power. Understand, however, that decreeing balance is a stopgap and cannot be sustained. All fingers are needed for balance to be sustained.

Consider awareness. Most, if not all, awareness activities must have authorization and resources. They need real standing. Leadership, or whoever the authority may be, must stand up and say, "Make it so." Otherwise, the best campaigns may only be pieces of paper posted to wall, and the best training that once lived in a classroom can quickly die in the hallways.

I and many others have been involved in webinars that had little or no attendance. I and many others have put out newsletter articles and social media posts that went unheeded if not altogether unread or unheard. And I and many others have conducted countless other awareness activities that have been met with "So what?" It is up to authority to answer the "So what?" not in terms of content or context, but in terms of intent and impact.

If your organizational leadership wants the entire organization to know that gender balance is good for all, that a culture of safety is the culture to create, that female inclusion should be watched for and enabled, and that allies are needed, then leadership must say so.

Any efforts at trying to get that message out without some type of authority would be like broadcasting with the volume set very low. Authority turns up the volume.

Authority is needed to ensure safety also. More than anything safety is a matter of culture. Leadership should take ownership in establishing safe culture, whether that leadership is male, female, a combination of individuals, or a specific group. Leadership, or whoever is the authority, decrees a culture of safety in a number of ways, perhaps the biggest of which is accountability.

One place where accountability should be decreed and reiterated often is with rule of law. Recall Title VII, for example. Imagine such a law being set in place without authority. When it comes to rules, authority is added to rule via accountability. Those who fail at upholding the rules suffer consequence via authority.

But while most would agree that rules work when accountability is in place, it must also be understood that accountability can't exist without authority. Imagine a professional basketball game. Most understand there are rules in place to limit fouls that occur when someone is physically overly aggressive toward another player. There is accountability in the form of penalty. The referee enforces the accountability for breaking the rules. But what if the referees stopped showing up? Sure, for a while the game would remain intact, but it would eventually degenerate. The effectiveness of the game would be lost.

Rules are made living instruments of change and impact with active and consistent authority. For example, authority may be represented by leaders who stand up and say these are the rules, and there will be zero tolerance of rule mitigation in any way, shape, or form. Only when authority holds tightly to the rules and raises them to be both visible and useful will others see them in the correct light and apply or adhere to them appropriately.

Zero tolerance is a good example to use, as it states consistency. Consistency is entirely necessary. Consistency comes from standing by the rules and remaining ever cognizant of those rules and their use or nonuse.

Things will not change where there is flippancy.

Safety will not occur in cultures of flippancy. Authority and flippancy are mutually exclusive.

As with a culture of safety based on rules to which people are held accountable, a culture of inclusion that is founded on practices and programs also is dependent on authority and accountability.

Inclusive practices are very often products of culture, and they are oftentimes grassroots efforts. Anytime a culture or practice is generated by grassroots efforts, it is a good thing. Things born of grassroots efforts are likely the most appropriate to the environment and what people want to see in that environment for themselves. It could be said that grassroots efforts provide their own authority. But understand that such authority is limited, and grass won't grow tall where limited.

Consider a practice whereby the number of men and women are accounted for when setting up meetings or conferences. Such a practice could actually become part of the culture—done by reflex more so than by procedure. However, the first time a real authority shows up and says that it is not necessary—*poof*, out the window that practice goes. Such an occurrence may be only be an isolated incident, but even isolated incidents causes stagnation of a practice over time. With authority backing practice from the beginning, however, the practice is in effect is locked into place. That doesn't mean grassroots efforts are not good, but it does mean grassroots efforts need real authoritative backing in some form.

I likewise advocate that programs can, and should, originate in grassroots efforts. But even the best of grassroots programs won't last long without authority.

In the absence of grassroots efforts, leadership should put programs in place by decree. Certainly leadership can author, implement, and back inclusion programs, for example. Call it inclusion by decree if you like. Authoritarian decree may seem to contradict inclusion as a matter of a culture, and it may also seem more of a dictatorial methodology, but those are not wholly incorrect assessments. I'm not saying inclusion by decree is best; just that it is possible.

Vocalization of support is important. In whatever ways a practice or program is given initial authority, credibility is only secured through vocalization of support. Whoever represents authority must ensure that such programs and practices are known and understood, and they also must ensure that implementation is handled correctly. It's not that the authority has to do all the legwork themselves, but they do need to take responsibility in seeing these things done.

Allies are the last of the means for organizations to adjust the scales. One might ask "What does authority have to do with allies?" It certainly could be questioned whether or not you can have allies by decree. But yes, you can. Allies can be decreed and actually are decreed in a great many organizations. Recall the previous discussion around ERGs, for example. Most, if not all, ERGs are put into place by leadership or some other authority. The same is true of some circles. Champions, too, can be products of authority.

Furthermore, understand that decree does not have to be formal. If an authority stands before those in the organization and declares that allies of women are needed, and if that authority is truly an authority, at least some will take note and take heed.

In fact, there are many ways authority can make declarations that foster balance.

Balance by Decree

To decree balance or elements thereof, leaders or authorities might start with very vocal proclamations that attest to the commitment of leadership on behalf of the organization. This could take the form of a code of ethics, for example.

> **Code of Ethics for our employee family and those we serve**
>
> This company values a healthy space where all employees feel safe, free from harm, and free to excel as unique, valued, and respected individuals. To that end, all employees will operate consistent with the following principles.
>
> - We commit to being responsible to the people and stakeholders who use our products and services.
>
> - We commit to operate with the highest standard of integrity and strive to foster trusting relationships with all.
>
> - We commit to always be ethical in our communications with those we serve and our employees. Communication and conduct in all forms will be held to the highest of standards of civility, respectfulness, truthfulness, accuracy, completeness, honesty, and transparency.
>
> - We reject any act or communication that is disparaging, violent, intimidating, or harassing and/or expresses hatred or intolerance of our employees, partners, and those we serve. This company has zero tolerance for harassment of any kind against anyone.

- We commit to being responsible to all of our workforce and all of our stakeholders.

- We acknowledge that respectful and nonbiased treatment of our employees is not a choice; it's the law. We promote equality of opportunity and treatment for all regardless of gender, race, ethnic or national origin, religion, age, marital status, sexual orientation, or disability. We will ensure that all laws and regulations that provide equal opportunity for all Americans are enforced.

- We likewise ask our partners, stakeholders, customers, and all entering this facility to join us in adhering to this code.

Again, there is a strong case to be made that this type of thing should not exclusively be product of leadership but more a grassroots effort. Getting more people involved in the formation of such declarations and guidelines has the advantages of multidiverse input into the product and greater potential buy-in versus being just another thing pushed down from management.

In any case, in looking at the example wording, notice how specific security, inclusion, and empowerment language is merged with general statements about company ethical practices.

Gender Mainstreaming (Again)

Recall the usefulness of gender mainstreaming as an overall strategy. Gender mainstreaming codifies gender sensitivity into actions the organization can undertake to achieve gender-sensitive effectiveness. In so doing, gender mainstreaming can operate as an instrument to establish goals for participation and influence. Some of these can be numbered goals, such as work group or meeting participation ratios. A non-numbered goal, for example, may be to ensure both a member of this sex and a member of that sex are final sign-off authorities for any new position description. Codification can take place with such publicized goals or can be inserted into strategic plans.

It could be said that codification follows decree. Again, gender mainstreaming as an initiative could be forged as a grassroots effort. Or it might be simply an authoritarian decree. We've dealt with the pros and cons of origination of such initiatives earlier in this chapter, so we'll focus more on an authority, any authority, using such formalized means to the goal of gender balance.

Large and documented initiatives like these could be seen in a sense to carry authority unto themselves. They represent authority. They are a master plan in the sense of their overarching role.

In the case of gender mainstreaming, one analogy is that gender mainstreaming is like a restaurant's kitchen from which products are created. Gender mainstreaming as a kitchen is composed of things like stoves, ovens, microwaves, and sinks—being analogies to the other essential elements, which in the case of gender balance might be awareness, security, inclusion, and allies. The kitchen is the overarching component in this analogy. Or it might be seen as container of the other elements. In any case the kitchen rules. The oven has no place out on its own.

If gender balance were a delicious meal, gender mainstreaming would indeed be the kitchen.

Officially, gender mainstreaming is the (re)organization, improvement, development, and evaluation of policy processes so that a gender equality perspective is incorporated into all policies at all levels and at all stages by the actors normally involved in policy making. Gender mainstreaming is not a goal in itself, but a strategy to achieve equality between women and men. It involves a process of change and transformation that implies all actors involved in policy making integrate gender equality concerns. This means integrating a systematic consideration of the differences between the conditions, situations, and needs of women and men; the relations existing between them; and the differentiated policy impact on the concrete lives of women and/or men in the planning, implementation, monitoring and evaluation of all policies, programs, and activities. This policy strategy also aims to have both sexes influence, participate in, and benefit equitably from all interventions. The main goal of gender mainstreaming is to enable both sexes to enjoy equal visibility, empowerment, and participation in all spheres of public and private life.

If you look at the language, the words *influencing* and *participating* should jump out as part and parcel of how gender balance has been defined in this book. Ultimately, gender mainstreaming instills gender considerations into plans, policies, services, and education that affect the contributions and influence of men and women in all things.

Gender mainstreaming differs significantly from other gender-equality approaches.

- Gender mainstreaming is entirely concerned with gender as it applies equally to the concerns and experiences of both men and women.
- Gender mainstreaming can be applied at all levels of organizations, businesses, and governments.
- Gender mainstreaming does not require legislation or even policy.
- Gender mainstreaming is proactive. It is applied in the planning and decision-making stages rather than in implementation and reaction.

Another difference is that while gender balance is concerned with the balanced internal workings of a work group, gender mainstreaming is applied both to internal organizational workings as well as to external products and services.

Our concern here is with the internal workings of the organization. But the same use of gender mainstreaming applies. As an internal issue, gender mainstreaming ensures that women and men have equal participation, equal access to and control over resources, and equal input into decision-making. With proper implementation, gender mainstreaming is authority over balance.

Gender Action Plan

Another approach to codifying gender balance goals, documenting them, and giving them authority is creating a gender action plan. Here again I will say this can be done by decree, but it may be better as a grassroots effort. Begin by documenting what can be done in the interest of gender balance (contribution and influence parity). Involve others to add ideas, best practices, and information. Share gender plans and documents.

A gender action plan is one of the best ways to begin formalizing gender balance activities and initiatives. A gender action plan is a living document that is an impetus for action and a tool for accountability. A gender action plan identifies programs and activities that improve gender balance. It can list, for example, anti-harassment campaigns, trainings, gender events, implementation of new gender policies and procedures, recruiting initiatives, instillment of new gender-supporting roles, creation of gender-supporting documents and tools, and so on.

There are a number of selling points for utilizing gender action plans. For one, they tend to imply action versus a static position. Second, they can assign responsibility. Third, each item can be tracked individually. And finally, a gender action plan is dynamic and can be modified as needed—and it should be modified and maintained as a living document of action.

The document should include the following.

- Items to improve balance (plan, policy, program, activity). Be sure to include items that together address awareness, security, inclusion, allies, and empowerment. In identifying implements of balance, include the why with the what, or the why can be a separate element in the document. Identify what the beneficial outcomes will be. A short statement of why puts the importance of what is being done front and center. The items and the why should be tied to and integrated with other formal organizational processes such as strategic plans and budget. This not only legitimizes the items and the gender action plan, it also helps with gaining attention, prioritizing, resourcing, and so on.

- A time frame for implementation. This is important for accountability.

- Priorities. Assign each item a priority. Sort the items, or merge priorities with timeframe information. Assigning priorities makes the plan doable so as not to take on too much at once.

- Responsible parties. This is necessary for ownership and accountability and might include two pieces: the person(s) or group responsible for implementing an item and the owner or sponsor of the item. Remember to consider the organizational position of the owner/sponsor. An executive high in the organization may have more power to put behind the item, but a lower-level leader might be able to give the item much better attention.

- Resources required (and/or other necessities and considerations for implementation). This includes money, staff, and so on. It can also include items such as identifying a needed owner/sponsor, making space within current educational curriculum, X number of hours of data gathering, and so on. Be realistic. Do not underestimate.

Gender equality statements, plans, and policies create authority, legitimacy, and accountability. Another benefit of either of these documents is that examples can be found easily and modified and tailored for the organization quickly. Because documents like these are common, their relative familiarity may ease acceptance.

In any declarations, be sure to use active versus passive language. Make the documents read as things that must be done as opposed to things you would like to see. In releasing the documents, spend the time and make the effort to explain why they are being included in the organizational culture. Following the release, analyze the understanding and acceptance of what you're trying to accomplish.

Regardless of the kind of formalized document used to set an organization on a leveling path, authorship should be a huge consideration. Higher-positioned authors have more power, but a grassroots endeavor with employee teams as author or involved as authors may give the document more credibility. You might ask who has the right knowledge to put into the document. Grassroots efforts may seem potentially less effective because they don't have the power leadership has; however, I've found that many leaders don't want to take on gender. If they do, they do so as matter of legal protection or appearance. Individuals may have to take responsibility themselves. And that is fine as long as authority is also given with the responsibility.

I've now presented all five of fingers of balance manipulation. The scale can be adjusted with these. The question is, does it take all five? The answer is yes, to some measure, anyway. But that does not mean they are all equal. I started this chapter by saying authority is the thumb. And am sticking by that here.

Chapter 11

Empowerment

We know that balancing the scale can be done by adding numbers to the lesser side. A second option is manipulation of the scale (the five fingers of manipulation).

The third means of balancing a scale is to somehow increase the weight of what is already present. In doing so we are increasing value (not numbers). Weight, or value, is increased by making better use of, better leveraging, or better appreciating what is already present. This weight increase can be—and arguably should be—done at the hands of the organization. Or it can be a matter of self-empowerment, as will soon be discussed. But, we begin in this chapter by looking at the former.

Weight (value) will be increased through empowerment. And while empowerment functions as a value increaser, a process separate from manual scale adjustment described previously, there are nonetheless links between the two. Empowerment cannot exist without security, inclusion, allies, and arguably awareness. A person cannot be empowered or feel empowered in an unsafe, unsettled, or uncomfortable environment. And empowerment cannot exist when people are excluded, silenced, or sidelined. Participation must be allowed before growth, development, and empowerment can take place. And no one can do it alone. It takes allies. It could also be argued that empowering systems will not be put into place without awareness. Thus, while empowerment alone can raise value, movement of the scale might still be limited without at least some of the other organizational adjustments.

In any case, empowerment is a direct path to increasing one's value.

It does have a direct effect on the scale, moving it toward balance. Empowerment adds value to women and also raises the value of everyone in an organization.

Empowerment Training

Perhaps the most widely recognized means to increase one's value is through training. Training is an empowerment tool that not only improves skills but expands capacity toward balance.

The best training is not done willy-nilly. Too often it is used in a shotgun approach, a very broad, one-size-fits-all approach. It should instead be very focused and targeted. Women's leadership training is an example—it is empowerment training with a specific goal that specifically targets women.

In my practice I'm often challenged by men as to why women should get leadership training that they may not. Of course, we know that it is warranted, as there are far more places where women are disempowered or devalued than where men are. The playing field is not level. Men typically have the better positions, which means they have the playbook to the game. In fact, they wrote the book.

Empowerment education is often focused on and especially effective in the area of leadership, because this is where many women struggle for reasons outlined earlier (minority status, devaluation, lack of opportunity, discrimination). If nothing else, empowerment education can be seen as a way to level the playing field.

A number of large and small organizations I have worked with recognize that female-targeted empowerment education directly empowers women, increases their value, and is a good organizational investment. The outcomes are enhanced capacity and improved organizational performance. There is always a positive return on investment (ROI) in terms of the benefits of balance. The ROI formula can be computed many ways and includes how the training itself is conducted and its associated costs.

Here is a successful three-day model:

Day 1: Hurdles and issues faced by women
 [self-evaluation and/or self-enrichment homework]
Day 2: Communications and leadership
Day 3: Private coaching sessions

The day 1 focus is on the playing field. The agenda includes discussion of male-centric environments as well as associated biases and other ramifications of being female in such environments. There is much eye-opening the first day. While there are many "of course" moments and few surprises for some women, there are new realizations or "aha" moments for others. The training includes means to cope with imbalanced situations and an even greater focus on means to succeed. By afternoon, there is a shift to an awakening of self-awareness in preparation for self-enhancement. Women recognize their own unique strengths and discuss ways to leverage those strengths. Homework may be assigned at the end of the day to further self-awareness as a tool of self-enhancement.

Day 2 is about imparting new skills or bettering current ones with an emphasis on skills that can do the most toward leveling the playing field, plugging skills gaps, and expanding capacity. As we discussed earlier, these skills include communications, especially those communications situations where women may struggle, as well as the use of leadership styles in ways appropriate to the situation. The goal is not to make women better skilled than their male counterparts but rather to improve women's skills so that they are as valued as men and utilized fully to realize parity.

Individual coaching sessions are extremely valuable as a day 3 activity (or at any subsequent time). Knowledge gained in days 1 and 2 can be incorporated into practical problem-solving for a situation the coached participant may face or is presently facing. The facilitator, working as coach, works through the specific issue. The issue could be a problem with a superior, co-worker, or subordinate; difficulty getting a project resourced; or working out a path to promotion. Alternatively, coaching sessions can be worked into a group setting to determine group solutions to participants' issues.

Empowerment training is never exclusive of men. When people ask whether men should participate in female empowerment trainings, I always answer yes. For one thing, men need to be involved in all solutions to female disempowerment. Additionally, there is great value in including both male and female perspectives in discussions, because everyone can take away valuable information and insights. But it should also be noted that many women feel uncomfortable with male attendance in such situations, and many will not fully participate with men in the room. Such discomfort and hesitancy to participate can greatly hinder training, so participants' wishes must be considered and may warrant accommodation. While I advocate men's involvement, I certainly fully support the worth of female-only classes as well. A third choice is a hybrid approach in which women have a day to themselves and men join on the second day. Nearly any kind of split is workable.

The idea of mixed-gender classes brings us to a topic we discussed earlier: cross-gender skills training. Such training is an organizational imperative. If an organization wishes to fully reap the performance benefits of balance, then the organization must enhance the skill sets of both men and women. For men, that often means learning skills that may not have been a personal or organizational priority for them. Many men don't see the need to modify their skill sets to begin with, and that is especially in regard to skills (typically feminine skills) the organization does not value as evidenced by awards and evaluations. An organization should reward the acquisition and use of broadened skill sets, especially cross-gendered skill sets and take responsibility for making that happen. Of course, many organizations do offer cross-skills and soft-skills training as part of regular team and leadership trainings, but few back it up with performance metrics that ensure application.

Cross-gender skills training is not terribly different from either empowerment training (usually targeted to women) or soft-skill trainings usually framed within general team and leadership courses. If an organization already has those types of training offerings, then it doesn't have a lot of work to do. The organization will likely insert some gender instruction into the existing curriculum as appropriate—issues and impacts items, for example. Think of the skills training as the present. Then remember the need to look at the before and the after, the background and the effect. New pieces must be added to the curriculum to incorporate male and female perspectives and considerations related to the skills. That is not to say that a man might use some skill like empathy or feedback differently from the way a woman might use it. They may or may not. More importantly, the issues around use of empathy or feedback may differ for a man or a woman, and the effects related to use of empathy or feedback may differ for a man or a woman. Also remember that much of the situation is contingent upon the existing environment in regard to gender makeup, gender expectations, gender history, and so on. For example, it is good to discuss that in some environments empathy can be seen as weakness in a man while it is more acceptable for a woman, or there may be cultural resistance to women giving certain types of direct feedback while it is accepted for men to do so. Discussing the pros and cons of empathy or the when, where, how, and why of empathy can benefit everyone.

This kind of training must be based on the specific environment at hand. If an organization denies that gender differences are a big part of work processes, and thus practices one-size-fits-all use of skills, it won't work as well. The more difference is addressed, however, the sooner parity can be brought about.

While cross-gender training is best conducted with men and women together, it doesn't have to be. For example, it may be part of female-empowerment training. Regardless of class makeup or format, the most important thing is that gender is a component. Gender will be a part of the environment regardless, so it makes little sense to leave it out of training.

Mentoring

A person could see how mentoring is a means of educating also. Most people understand how mentoring, in adding weight (value) to improve balance, can help an individual, especially a minority one.

Many organizations see mentoring as a go-to fix. That is not to say mentoring is the only fix, or even the best.

The problem is that in seeing mentoring as *the* fix, organizations fail to offer the necessary spectrum of support systems or even advocate them. I do discourage such a shortsighted view of mentoring and reliance on it to the exclusion of other additional fixes. While mentoring is certainly an essential cog in the machine of staff improvement, it is still only one cog.

Whenever mentoring is employed, it would be helpful to see that it is not only a means to give a person valuable information to help them advance their career, but that it is also a process that empowers and improves a person's value.

Mentors play the role of adviser, someone who can help with one's career or a specific work project. A mentor is a source of wisdom and support. A mentor may help explore career options, set goals, develop contacts, identify resources, and encourage perseverance, among other things. Many organizational leaders, female and male, are well aware of the plusses of mentoring, but not all of them do what is needed to instill successful mentoring programs that help balance the workplace.

Mentoring is especially important for women.

Only 54% of women overall have access to senior leaders who can act as mentors or formal sponsors.[65]

Lack of mentoring and lack of training are two of the top factors that limit many women. As we noted earlier, women don't get good feedback from their employers even though they ask for it. On average, women get helpful management feedback 20% less than men do. Mentoring could fill the gap and balance the scales.

Successful employees are groomed for success. As a part of a grooming process, mentors can advise on such things as education, work priorities, seeing and meeting cultural and performance expectations of leaders, communications best practices, decision-making practices, relational practices in working with and leading others, decorum, and so many other areas. Here again women are less likely to be groomed. One reason is their lack of mentoring relationships with higher-positioned individuals. Again, imbalanced male and female staffing ratios are a big factor in this.

A big shortfall in many mentoring programs is accounting for varying need during different career stages. One fallout of that oversight is a mismatch of mentors to mentees. For example, a mentor and a mentee may be too far apart in position. A mismatch may also result from a lack of understanding of present needs and concerns of the mentee.

For women, it is especially important that mentoring differs at different stages of their development.

For women, it is most important to get direct, hands-on mentoring early in their careers because that is when many women choose to opt out of the workplace because they are struggling to find their footing. Men opt out far less often to attend to family or pursue other interests. Men are much more likely to stick it out in the early years, so early career mentoring is not as important for them. The type of mentoring that men need most is at mid-career, to help keep them from stalling out. Seldom do mentoring programs adapt to differing employee needs in these types of ways.

Each person must take responsibility for finding the right mentor. One huge hindrance is self-imposed limitation on who would be an appropriate mentor. Both men and women should choose mentors based on what a potential mentor can do for them and not on how much a potential mentor thinks or looks like them.

My all-time favorite PowerPoint slide is one I show when I discuss mentors in my workshops. The slide includes a picture of Condoleezza Rice with this quote: "Never be afraid to try something hard even when you are not good at it. And don't think that your mentors have to look like you. Instead, your role models need to share your passion and be able to give you the best advice they can. My mentors have been old white men. If I had waited for a black woman Soviet specialist, I might still be waiting."

Too many women do themselves a disservice by looking exclusively for female mentors.

For one, female mentors can be harder to find, especially in male-majority workplaces and institutions. More importantly, in most places, men are in more power positions and possess more information, which can be an asset. Enlightened men are critical to the success of women.

Here are other good reasons for women to consider male mentors.

- Male mentors have proved to be as effective for female mentees as female mentors.

- Male mentors likely have insider information.

- Female mentees often develop an inferiority complex with successful women.

- Female mentors more often than male mentors encourage women to quit and pursue other interests.

These considerations are not free from counterargument, however.

- Male mentors may back off or lower expectations for women. For some male mentors, this is a product of being socialized to see women as more soft, fragile, or domestically minded than professionally minded. Men may underestimate women's abilities and resiliency.

- When men mentor women, they advise them to build networks.

When men mentor men, they advise them to focus on strategy. Strategy is a much broader approach that can include mentoring and many other elements of empowerment as well. The difference in advised approaches can be the result of misunderstanding the needs of women, disinterest, or underestimation.

- Female mentors are in a position to take on female issues. For example, female mentors can work to dispel the myth of the exceptional female.

Men, too, need mentors. Those who have mentored me, both formally and informally, have assisted greatly in my professional progression in advancement in ability and advancement in position. Some helpful women have been among my mentors as well. Furthermore, according to a 2009 Catalyst study, men who have female mentors also say they've had their eyes opened to gender equity issues.[66]

All my mentoring relationships, male and female, have been professionally fulfilling as well as personally and emotionally fulfilling. In short, they have been good for me in both regards, and I'm grateful for the experiences.

For men, there are big plusses to being in a mixed-gender mentor/mentee relationship.

For one, such a relationship may offer a unique perspective and possibly generate new lines of thinking. It can also help men understand issues women face. From an organizational perspective, cross-gender awareness is a huge requisite to balancing the workplace.

Cross-gender mentoring is a plus for everyone. Both sexes benefit in terms of sharing skill sets and knowledge, and this is especially true when it comes to balance and the transfer of cross-gender skills. It helps foster balance.

To benefit most from the experience, both parties must be fully committed to giving time and attention to the relationship and being open. Mentors need to be fully willing to share their knowledge, skills, and expertise and to help and advise for the long-term benefit of the mentee and the entire company. The mentee must be fully open to advice. That doesn't mean the mentee only listens and takes. The mentee should listen and accept advice, but they should also analyze the advice for correct application to current workplace need. Mentoring should be done in partnership to find agreed-upon logistics and agreed-upon goals. Mentees should not allow their mentors to stray off track or distract attention and energy from the agreed-upon goals. Mentors should be held to task. Women, especially, should ensure that male mentors remain strategic in partnership with the mentee's goals.

If mentors are several ranks above their mentees, they could be less effective. Mentors and mentees can be peers. Although peer mentors do not necessarily have insights that might elevate a person to a higher position, they do likely have insights into the mentee's current position that the mentee may not have considered. Mentees can have more than one mentor. As with networking, mentors ought to be varied in terms of diversity, position, and purpose.

Coaches

Coaching can be seen as a specific form of mentoring. Mentors and coaches might actually be seen as one and the same, and the terms are often used interchangeably. However, while similar in their support of someone's development, they are different disciplines in practice.

Mentoring is ongoing while coaching is situational or case by case. Coaching is typically a relationship with a finite duration with focus on strengthening or eliminating specific behaviors in the here and now. A mentor is not typically someone who observes and advises on specific actions or behavioral changes in daily work. Mentoring is a long-term relationship that focuses on supporting the growth and development of the mentee. Coaches may be temporarily engaged to help professionals correct behaviors that detract from their performance or strengthen those behaviors that support stronger performance around a set of activities. In short, you could say the focus of coaching is problem-solving. Though mentoring can target performance improvement, its primary purpose is career success and advancement. Some overlap with coaching will be seen, and repetitious coaching may evolve into mentoring.

The following examples may be helpful in differentiating coaching from mentoring. A coach teaches a baseball or softball pitcher how to improve a certain pitch or teaches a quarterback how to run a play. A mentor teaches a quarterback how to be a great quarterback and perhaps how to become a great football manager. In academia, a coach can help a professor with a problem student, new subject material, or working an administration issue. A mentor, on the other hand, will help a professor be a better professor overall and potentially become a dean or provost or even president.

If you thought I shortchanged the discussion of mentors, you may think I have shown even less love of coaching. Again, there is good reason. When it comes to organizational balance, the issue is the same. It is harder for the minority sex to find suitable coaches, and that's especially true if the person limits herself or himself to coaches of the same sex. Most of the issues that can hinder or help mentoring programs apply to coaching. And most of the same considerations apply to selecting coaches. Both mentoring and coaching are incredibly valuable, and both ought to be sought out with equal attention and consideration.

Many organizations know about and invest in mentoring programs, but far fewer do that with coaching as a separate service. Organizations should instill formal coaching programs as well as mentoring programs to fulfill the functions outlined above. In organizational balance, coaching programs are another cog in the gears that will help balance an imbalanced organization. Like mentoring, coaching can be extremely helpful to those not in power by adding to their ability to contribute and influence. For most organizations, that means finding coaches for women in the same ways mentors are found, with coaches as additional provisions rather than replacements.

Sponsors

Another cog in the leveling machinery is sponsorship programs, and it is arguably the most important cog. Studies show that people with sponsors are 23% more likely to move up in their careers than are those without sponsors. A sponsorship program is a direct leveling device as it directly increases weight (value).

Sponsoring can make huge differences. While mentoring focuses on feedback and advice, sponsoring is active influence and strategies for advancement.

Sponsors actively promote you or your cause and actively pull you up via opportunities for involvement.

While mentoring is like someone walking before you in the snow and leaving footsteps for you to follow, sponsoring is like someone putting you on a snowmobile with them and speeding forward. In differentiating mentors from sponsors, sponsors need to be in positions of influence to make things happen and to be effective.

Returning to the movie *Hidden Figures*, Katherine Johnson could not have succeeded had it not been for the elevating intervention of Al Harrison. Harrison was in a position of influence and not only gave her advice but also took active and intentional steps to ensure she was included in processes.

As depicted in the movie *Iron Lady*, real-life male member of Parliament Airey Neave reached out to Margaret Thatcher when she first arrived as a new, 33-year-old member of Parliament in 1959. Neave took Thatcher fully under his wing in the all-male House of Commons and showed her the ropes. Over time, he became a trusted adviser as well as her campaign manager on her way to becoming prime minister.

These are true depictions of what an actual sponsor does. In looking at the second example, you could say Neave was a mentor or a coach. But Neave went beyond advice; he actively promoted Thatcher through introductions and invites. Like Neave, sponsors introduce the person being sponsored to influential people; tout the person's skills, knowledge, and accomplishments; invite the person into meetings; and so on.

One of the most powerful actions by a sponsor is providing a seat at the table for women through invitations to meetings, conferences, and trainings. Only then do they get the kind of exposure needed to advance themselves and their ideas.

Earlier in this chapter, I mentioned women are less likely to be groomed for management positions because they don't have mentoring relationships with officials already in those posts. I qualified the statement by adding that it's true in part. To make the statement whole, I'll add that women do not have sponsor relationships with influential officials. Sponsorship itself is imbalanced.

In many organizations, even where women are being mentored, it is still men who are being sponsored.

This is largely due to the fact that social groups often fall along gender lines. Men associate more often with men, and women associate more often with women. Again, in most places men are in the power (sponsor potential) positions. Bias, conscious or unconscious, may also be a contributing factor that causes men to sponsor more men than women.

Women in power might also decline sponsoring other women, assuming that since they themselves made it with little help, so too should other women. Similarly, in sponsoring men in need, some leaders of either sex might assume the playing field is level or favors men, so men don't need help. Depending on the type of imbalance present, these can be wrong and harmful assumptions.

In any case, sponsoring is more freely given to men by men. Many men don't even have to ask to be sponsored. Many female employees, on the other hand, are in dire need of sponsoring. If that describes you, you will likely have to ask to be sponsored. Make a point of doing so. And my advice to men is this: do your part. Bring women to the table; be sponsors to all in need. If you are an organizational leader, in addition to the other cogs, strongly consider how you can make sponsorship a part of your balancing strategy.

Role Models

In talking about others who can assist in one's empowerment, I wish to also talk about role models and how they may differ from mentors and how beneficial they can be. One study found that subtle exposure to highly successful female leaders improves women's performance in leadership tasks.

When people are shown photographs of other people in other roles (e.g., doctor, police officer) and then asked to list their own traits, people often note traits most commonly associated with the picture they were shown. More importantly, they subsequently exhibited those traits. In an example of this, women behave more tenderheartedly when they think of themselves as wives or mothers rather than as salespeople. Something as simple as checking a male/female box (or flashing the word *male* or *female* for less than a second) primes an individual and affects performance and associations.

Watching role models perform can be powerful. It has been found that when women look at an image of a strong, positive female role model before they give an oral presentation, they present with a more confident demeanor and tone. In fact, they speak longer.

Observing other successful professionals, either in person or in videos, can be extremely helpful. Even reading about role models is useful.

Given their underdog status in many organizations, women can definitely benefit from strong, confident role models. Men can benefit and improve with role models as well.

But there are a couple of caveats that tend to affect women more.

For one, sometimes when women see another woman in a typically male-dominated role or field, rather than seeing that woman as a role model or even recognizing that it was simply not the norm for that position or field, they feel discomfort or a sense of rivalry. This is turn can lead to tug-of-war behaviors, as described previously. Furthermore, extremely successful role models can make success seem unattainable and cause others to devalue their own worth by comparison.

High-level female role models might very well negatively affect women's self-perceptions and leadership aspirations. This is especially true for younger women, who are more likely to lack confidence. Again, this is an organizational concern. It is difficult for women to find role models in imbalanced organizations and even more difficult to find role models who appropriately inspire. The fewer members of one's own sex in an organization, the less likely there will legitimate role models.

The situation can be dire for women in male-dominated fields and industries. Many women yearn for role models and search far and wide to find them. I have seen this profoundly in coaching women internationally. Some women who are rare representatives of their sex in their male-dominated profession come into a workshop and are excited to see for the first time other women who could be role models for them. Some of these extremely intelligent women have never seen another woman at their level or above, let alone a woman they can admire and aspire to become. The positive impacts are immediate.

How can we expect people to succeed when they can't see any evidence that such success is possible? Individuals can't be responsible for finding role models. That is the organization's responsibility. Organizations would do well to:

- Make role models more visible. Put them in newsletters, on posters, on social media, at the lectern, at conferences, at meetings, at banquets.

- Make role models more available in person to individuals and groups.
- If role models are not readily available, reach out and identify role models outside the immediate environment. Borrow role models—even virtual role models.
- Work at identifying mid-level female role models who will encourage rather than discourage young women.

These might not seem like big things, but they have great effect.

As a last caveat about role models, remember the Rudy Giuliani story I related earlier. While it is good to admire role models (Winston Churchill, in Rudy's case), it is not good to emulate them. The goal is not to emulate your role models. Rather, the goal is to learn from your role models.

Role models help stretch a person's confidence. Another, and quite direct, means to stretch a person is through tasking.

Tasking and Stretch Assignments

Another means to achieve better balance is to modify the way tasks are allocated. Good assignments and bad assignments should be handed out equitably. A manager can create a fair turn-taking system or random assignment of tasks rather than relying on people volunteering. Women are more often tasked with things of little value and return, so a manager should encourage male staff to volunteer for such tasks. Another thing that a manager can do is to create stretch assignments that challenge and help grow an individual's skills and knowledge and that increase a person's capacity and improve their odds for advancement. Stretch assignments need to doled out equitably as enablers of parity. These can be great ways for male managers and male staff to signal their alliance with women colleagues.

My favorite saying in teaching team leadership is "The person who sweeps the floor ought to be able to select the broom." If you are a leader with hiring authority, I hope you hire staff based on talents and skills. Empowerment is letting people use their unique skills and talents fully.

It's allowing people to take full responsibility for work—both how the work is done and the results. This is especially important to undervalued people in imbalanced organizations. When the undervalued are given opportunities to stretch themselves, they ought to also be given the freedom to approach the work in the ways they know best.

One thing that holds up empowerment is the requirement of a leader to let go.

Many leaders don't let go because of stubbornness, ego, and fear, and more male leaders than female leaders do this. Recall that there is a time and place for all leadership styles. Delegation is perhaps the most important one. Letting go is hard for many leaders, but very necessary.

In empowering women in this way, understand it is not about giving women chances but rather providing opportunities. The former implies that women might be able to do as well as men but suggests little confidence in them doing so, let alone bettering men at the task. The latter is more literal in word, intent, and practice.

Do not set women up for failure. Do not make women expendable, and don't put them in a position to fall on a sword. The tasking must be important and have a reasonable chance and expectation of success. Women's presence must be purposeful and not tokenism. Women need the resources and power to succeed.

Expectations should not be set low. Stretch assignments should legitimately challenge women. It doesn't have to be comfortable. Challenge is needed for growth.

And finally, make ample opportunities. Recall that women need to work 2.5 times harder to receive the same recognition—thus there is need to give more opportunities to women.

Resourcing

Resourcing is another means of empowerment, one that very much demonstrates leadership's commitment to maximizing contribution and influence—the proverbial putting one's money where their mouth is. Part of resourcing is funding, for example, for training. Gender empowerment can be resourced in many ways.

When my children were at home, our family participated frequently in community theater productions. When my daughter was young, she was a quiet little girl. She enjoyed being on stage, but she enjoyed being backstage more. With her quiet nature, she didn't often initiate anything or take charge—until she was empowered with the right tools. The empowerment tool for her was a headset and microphone, which transformed her backstage presence from follower to leader. She barked orders to any and all, regardless of age or standing. The empowering tools literally gave her voice.

Maybe an empowering tool is a microphone, or maybe it's a new piece of software or a computer or even the right arrangement of the right office furniture in the right location. These tools can be big, small, or both. Certainly, it can be empowering to be given a staff, as another example. A corporate credit card is empowering, though it might seem a small thing. Size is not the issue. Tools of empowerment can be anything that enables performance or development or simply demonstrates organizational confidence.

Resourcing can be seen as a sign of being valued, a psychological benefit beyond the tool itself. The providing of resources increases confidence. They can be the spinach to the person's inner Popeye. Sometimes seeing the possibility of empowerment helps realize empowerment. Empowerment is both supplied and self-induced.

This is a good time to note a thinking trap: the trap of thinking that *equitable* means the same (equal) treatment for all. To serve balance, leadership must embrace the notion that equality does not necessarily mean equal.

Oftentimes, in the interest of balance, some people need things from the organization that others do not.

This may cause pushback, because some will see this as giving to some and not others, or perhaps as favoring one sex over the other. Anticipate the pushback and be prepared to deal with it. Leadership must be transparent with no attempt to circumvent. Most importantly, make sure the why is clear and clearly understood. Whether it is training, tasking, or resourcing, the goal is parity in contribution and influence, not parity in allocation of things. By increasing one person's value, everyone and the organization benefits.

I will also add that good solutions, like good clothes, are never one-size-fits-all. They are best when they are tailored for an individual. Capacity expansion can and should be targeted to empower the undervalued on a case-by-case basis. Giving a person more training when what they really need is opportunity to perform a new challenging role or assignment may miss the mark for further empowerment. On the other hand, throwing someone into a difficult assignment before they are prepped with needed training also misses the mark. And empowering a person with an assistant or a budget is not good if there is nothing challenging to assist with or nothing that needs to be bought that would expand the capacity of anyone or the organization. Consider the right empowering tool on a per person basis.

Individual Development Plans

A number of organizational means to raise value were discussed in this chapter. Many of them could be called individual development. Many organizations use formal individual development plans, and I recommend that highly. The plans should be tailored as much as possible and should include many of the things we discuss throughout this book.

Individualized plans operate on at least two levels. On one level, they help identify things that can and should be done in the interest of raising individual value. On another level, they instill accountability to make those things happen.

Far too often, individual development plans are filled out, signed by the employee and the manager, and then filed out of sight and out of mind. We need a new way to look at individual development plans. There may be a marketing solution here, or perhaps a branding solution. A leader may, for example, rename these personal development paths, which may help emphasize personal responsibility. The word *path* implies some level of organization and strategy versus haphazard or check-the-box action. I like personal empowerment plans because the word *empowerment* gains attention. It answers one of the main questions about motivation: what's in it for me? And empowerment represents the core of balance and parity toward increasing value.

There are many ways to empower. The important thing here is that these things need to be formalized, institutionalized, or owned by leadership. Take mentoring, coaching, and sponsoring initiatives, for example. These are means to support, expand capacity, and empower. They must not only be formally instilled in the workplace, but they must receive backing at every level of the organization. For one thing, an organization could make mentoring a requirement of every manager. Mentoring goals should be part of organizational success metrics that leadership is accountable to. Tailored mentoring plans could be put into place for all employees, especially the underrepresented in imbalanced workplaces. Gender champions should be fostered, supported, and rewarded.

Empowerment is a commitment, one that likely comes with sacrifice. But empowerment is also an investment. It's an investment in raising the value of an individual. And there is without a doubt high return on that investment.

I want to close this chapter with a plug for self-empowerment

When I first left government service and wanted to take my message of non-numbers-bound balancing public, I naturally had many conversations with various people in the industry. One of those conversations was with an event coordinator who was booking me into a number of conferences. I explained my message in full, including the five fingers, empowerment, and individual self-empowerment. I noted scale manipulation on behalf of both the organization, but also noted that sometimes individuals have to take the responsibility of weight (value) raising into their own hands. It was on the latter I got pushback. The man said to me, "Wait a minute, Dave. If the playing field is not level, or the organization imbalanced, isn't it leadership's responsibility to fix that?"

The answer is yes, of course it is. And that is why I wrote this book. However, leadership does not always fully satisfy its responsibility, or it may abdicate the responsibility altogether. The effort all too often falls on the individual.

I educate on both how an organization can balances the scales and how individuals can raise their own value.

In the first edition of this book, I included the topic as a chapter. However, I've since come to realize that only one chapter falls short in what needs to be said. So, I elected to move the topic to my next book—stay tuned.

As a starting point, or tease, I will say, however, that men and women need to focus on the following to raise their own value.

For women:
- Building confidence, taking risks, and finding grit
- Self-proclamation and gaining voice
- Navigating the expectation/authenticity balance
- Networking

For men:
- Situational awareness
- Communications—especially listening

In an unbalanced workplace, whatever an organization or yourself can do to increase your value goes a long way in tipping the scales through increased ability to contribute and influence.

Chapter 12

Balance by the Numbers

Aside from increasing the value of others and yourself, it has to be acknowledged that when it comes to both balance and power, the numbers can be quite significant. I hope it's been made clear that numbers are not a necessary means to achieve balance, but this does not mean that they are not a useful means.

Quotas

When it comes to gender balance, most people assume it to be about numbers. They may possibly consider it to be a hiring or promotion issue, but oftentimes such pondering quickly turns to the numbers, and from there to quotas. Quotas can occur in many forms. You may recall that some countries—Norway and Spain, for example—have enacted laws that prescribe balanced executive leadership. Regulations require that no more than 60% of a public corporation's board be made up of one gender. Likewise, some countries—India is an example—have laws requiring certain numbers when it comes to elections and public representation.

There is ample evidence that quotas are effective. And there are ample arguments that say they are fair given historical injustices, disparity, and inequalities. But there are counterarguments as well.

On the issue of effectives, quotas may effectively modify numbers to be more equal—but equal has nothing to do with effectiveness.

It can also be said that quotas set a bar—a low bar—that represents only a minimum rather than a bar of ideal and effectiveness.

On the issue of justice and fairness, they are too often argued to be subjective. And the issue is then argued on the semantics of equality versus equity. In the end, a debate on these things is not of large interest here, mostly as quotas are but one possibility of many to address the numbers problem.

Numbered Representation and Power

Our interest at this time is more focused on the effects of practices that can alter the numbers. Where possible, adding women (or men) to achieve balance via hiring or promotion can certainly work, because the numbers shift likely results in a power shift (but not always), and power allows for more contribution and influence parity.

Power is the ultimate goal, and numbers can certainly aid in that. *Aid* is a good word, or perhaps *tool* might be even more correct; The numbers are a tool or an aid to balance but are not a solution on their own.

Still, the numbers are not inconsequential. The fact is that they do count. (Pardon the pun.)

In imbalanced environments, women are disempowered by, or may disempower themselves through, disempowering stereotypical behaviors. Economist Robin J. Ely writes, "Women who worked at firms with a low number of women in power, sex roles were more stereotypical, and sex roles were more problematic."[67]

To address power imbalances, Sweden and other countries have recently passed laws that have made it illegal for corporate boards of directors to have more than 60% of one gender. This added a great number of female CEOs to boardrooms with resulting improved decision-making, communications, and so on.

Communications and decision-making influence are obviously big deals in the boardroom. These things are often key to success or failure. Here the rule of three is in play. When a board has only one woman, her opinion is given less weight than a man's. That changes dramatically when there are three women on that board. Such a tipping point might be seen solely outcome of numbers, but the improvement is not a result of the number of women but of a new balance of traits brought to the table and the leveraging in contribution and influence.

Optics

Gender imbalances have negative repercussions beyond internal power. As just one example, there is the image and the reputation of the organization. For any organization to appear inclusive, it must be visibly diverse. And it is best if such diversity appears at all levels of the organization. There are plenty of reasons to make a fuss over such appearances. Reasons include recruiting advantages, sales, receipt of contracts or grants, and so on, all of which affect the success of the organization.

I never advocate tokenism in any form. Rather, I staunchly advocate for inclusiveness and empowerment and the benefits derived thereof. However, it must be understood that even the appearance of imbalance has grave consequences for any organization. The worst may be that an imbalanced and/or non-inclusive perception of the organization perpetuates a strangling imbalance.

If an agency appears non-inclusive and imbalanced, it will have an extremely difficult time being the opposite in reality.

No one wants to be a minority to begin with, and especially so if an organization appears to favor one gender or another. This is a problem of perpetuation. However, a visibly balanced male-to-female employee ratio appears more gender diverse, and that appearance would aid in recruiting, for example. Of course, the same holds true when talking about race, ethnicity, age, or any facet of diversity.

It is also about internal optics. The perception of imbalance itself is important. When the power structure is heavily concentrated in one gender, it is harder for members of the other gender to be perceived as strong or even to perceive themselves so. The power group seems legitimate and the non-power group less so. When a person feels powerless they act so. The perception has a direct impact on performance. Again, the numbers can affect this positively or negatively.

But it is not, nor should it be, all about optics. If number balance is solely a matter of tokenism, that is not a solution and will likely have openly negative consequences that outweigh optics.

Recruiting, Hiring, Promotion, and Retention

The numbers should always be seen as part of a solution and not the only solution. When they're seen as part of an overall solution, the numbers deserve much attention. What follows is a list of practices that at a minimum warrant consideration.

Hiring:

- Have strategies for hiring underrepresented groups.
- Ensure that job descriptions do not use biased language.
- Use blind resume reviews.
- Mandate diverse candidate slates.
- Use clear and consistent criteria for evaluating candidates.
- Track gender representation in hiring.

Subsequent to hiring, a balance in numbers is product of evaluation and promotion. Again, a quick list of items to consider.

Promotion:

- Require clear objective evaluation metrics.
- Check/review promotion criteria for fairness and relevance.
- Set gender targets for promotion.
- Track gender representation in promotions.

In taking a closer look at these activities, let's start with hiring, perhaps the area with the most possibility of effecting change in balance.

Recruiting and hiring processes have many best practices. The best strategy for creating a diverse and thus effective workforce is to use blind procedures. Many organizations have turned to conducting job interviews in which the interviewee is visually hidden from the interviewer; for example, orchestra candidates going through blind auditions. Some organizations even disguise or modify voices in interviews. Something as simple as hiding a name on an application can remove gender bias, as multiple studies have proven. It is easy to see how these things can be more gender-neutral to one degree or another.

In creating diversity, don't hire for fit, something too many managers are guilty of. Like assimilation, which we discussed earlier, fit tamps down difference, uniqueness, and specialness. Fit is about homogeneity. We already now diverse groups outperform homogeneous groups every time, so why hire who is the same as everyone else?

Rather than telling my clients to hire for fit, I tell them to hire for "mis-fit" or gap. The goal of hiring should be to plug gaps in what is needed rather than repeat what's already present. If you're forming a choir, you obviously don't want all vocalists to sound the same. Diversity yields range. The same is true of hiring positions in any organization. The problem is that hiring for fit, consciously or unconsciously, often results in hiring the same—over and over again.

Managers often have the best intentions when they hire for fit. They accept it as a means of easy assimilation. A person who fits will automatically integrate. This thinking turns a blind eye to the downside of assimilation. Ignoring assimilation concerns often occurs because of an intent to use fit as means to more creative hiring. And in this there is an erroneous belief that hiring for fit is a means to look past static qualifications and get to the uniqueness of a person. Fit, however, actually yields more homogeneity than does hiring for gap as it repeatedly acquires sameness.

The University of Texas studied hiring practices within the university system to determine which was most effective at bringing in individuals who subsequently proved to be high performers. Many believe getting to know a candidate helps to better evaluate them. That is, open and flexible processes should be best. The UT study found, however, that the best selections were made from the job applications alone and relying on listed qualifications rather than on interviews or auditions.

It might be surmised from the UT study that bias is inevitable in the interview process, and that may be a correct conclusion. Women represent approximately 50% of the world population and attend college and enter the workforce in ever increasing numbers. Women currently account for 58% of bachelor's degrees and 60% of master's degrees awarded. So why are glass ceilings still unbroken and representation in a number of fields so imbalanced? Obviously, there is bias involved—the question is when and how. That question needs answered before solutions to overcoming bias can be implemented.

I could talk much more about recruiting and hiring strategies and practices, and these are the typical approaches most organizations use to address balance issues, but throughout this book I hoped to not dwell on the typical. In fact, I argued that the typical way of thinking was not getting the job done. My intent is to look beyond the obvious and the common to find new solutions previously unconsidered.

Societal Conditioning and Career Selection

A part of the reason for imbalanced numbers in the workplace is still societal conditioning and bias and insistence upon maintaining norms. Gender biases and stereotypes about women still seep into employment decisions. Stereotypically and traditionally, there are many who still see women as limited to clerical jobs, nursing, teaching, and so on. Furthermore, given societal presumptions that men are assertive and ambitious while women are pleasant and nurturing, it is no surprise that more women hold positions as nurses, elementary teachers, or social workers, while men are more likely to be found occupying positions as engineers, architects, and lawyers. These career tendencies can be seen as product of self-fulfilling prophecies.

A traditional, historically based, vocational view can be imagined as two subway cars joined together. One car represents traditional male-dominated jobs—for example, engineering—and the other represents traditional female jobs—caregiving, for example. Historically, all men boarded the engineering car, and most women, being in positions of less power, deferred to men's stature and stubborn positioning and boarded the second car. This was the norm year after year, stop after stop. With attrition, men and women left their cars, and occasionally there was movement between cars, with the rare woman boarding the first car and the rarer man boarding the second car. Over time, things began to change. More women pushed their way into first car, but most men held pat and continued to board the first car also. The first car, the engineering car, was the epitome of patriarchy for years. Men held firmly to their seats, and when they did make space, it was largely for other men. The women who boarded the crowded, male-dominated engineering car got in but seldom got a real seat—at least not without much effort. Gradually, the balance shifted ever so slightly, with women in greater numbers figuring out how to win space on the first car.

The resulting image is largely of the pushing and posturing on the first car, and we lose sight of the dynamics happening in the second car. The people in the second car, the caregiving car, largely held pat and were free of struggle. It never was a space issue. The second car had plenty of room and plenty of seats—for either sex. The problem with the second car was that it lacked value, real and perceived. Yet, if more people on the first car had simply opted for the second car, the struggle would be greatly lessened. Of course, many women have done and still do just that. But very few of the men do. The second car is painted pink and given a name: pink-collar jobs. These jobs are derided by men and even a few women. The color and the word *pink* are synonymous with being weak and having less value in our society.

But what if a number of men in this imaginary situation did voluntarily leave the first car? The result would not be pushing and bumping but rather balanced flow—equal numbers of men of women wandering onto either car in near equal numbers. To make that a reality, we need only get a number of men to opt for the second car. But they don't, and the primary reason is male social pressure. Pay is an issue, but only so long as the "pink" jobs are not as socially valued as the first car jobs. Much of this could be changed by men, of course, including leading men in the workplace. However, as it stands, men (women, too, by the way) give men funny looks when they board the second car. The second car is not yet made comfortable for men.

Until men are encouraged to ride the second car—actually enticed to go into caregiving professions, for example—and openly accepted there, the first car will remain crowded, seats will be at a premium, and men will still be sitting stubbornly and not giving way without a struggle.

And as a side effect, the pay structure continues to disfavor the second car.

Many parents still push their own agendas for their daughters and sons. While there is much movement to get girls into STEM, for example, there's been no movement to get men into jobs traditionally held by women. Doing that could make a lot of space for women in the first car. The reasons are deeply ingrained societal masculine and feminine ideals. Parents or society can be blamed for this if you like, but many of you reading this are parents, and all of you are otherwise part of society. How many of you reading this have pushed women to move to the second car but at the same kept mum about what jobs men might pursue?

Very few entities are seeing balance in this way and dealing with the "pink" jobs side of the coin. One exception is Norway. Norway has long been a leader in gender equality. But the country wants to go even further. An increasing number of men have now been given incentives and are taking up traditionally female jobs, especially in the nursing and childcare sectors. Incentives are exactly what is needed.

Governments are one thing, but what about our concern: organizations? Organizations need to combat this history and thinking and address the other side of the coin. As much as they may want to recruit and hire female engineers, they need to account for the space. Organizations can't have more female scientists and CEOs until we have more male caregivers. You can't move a great many women into the boardroom until it's okay for some men to be at the admin desk. Only so many majority-dominated jobs open each year.

Space for more women necessitates that either men are displaced through competition where there is little turnover or a number of men must voluntarily choose other careers.

In most environments, women are not only a minority, they are disadvantaged in the competition to begin with for a variety of reasons outlined previously. And many women are discouraged from these positions at the same time men are discouraged from giving them up.

Making space means getting more men to take up positions more traditionally held by women.

It can be a tough sell and will require some imaginative solutions to truly balance roles.

Individually, imbalance is perpetuated without societal or organizational push to change. It becomes self-fulling prophecy. More men pursue math because they believe themselves better at it, for example, since they have been told so. I will cite again the study where women and men were shown photographs of other people in other roles (e.g., doctor, police officer) and then asked to list their own traits. Recall that they often noted traits that are most commonly associated with the picture they saw. Their own self-concept changed. The more we see images of women engineers or male caregivers, the more it becomes acceptable on both conscious and unconscious levels.

Biases and traits are linked. They are both products of conditioning, and they both affect choices and behaviors. It might then be speculated that masculine and feminine traits can play a large role in career selection. They can and they do. For example, because empathy is evidenced in more women, it is more likely that women will select careers where empathy is an asset, such as caregiving. In fact, in the field of medicine, women choose pediatrics much more often than men do, and the result is imbalance in the field.

In studies of communal-style communities, such as kibbutzes, where people are entirely free to choose occupations and where gender neutrality is a goal, 70–80% of women still choose occupations in which they work with other people and children, especially caregiving and education. Men still gravitate to work in the fields, construction, and maintenance. Fewer than 18% of men cared to work with children or elderly.

Is this an anomaly? Statistics say that in richer countries with better education, more favorable gender laws, more equal pay, and more sociably acceptable mixing of genders in careers—in short, more free choices—leads to more women choosing non-masculine and non-male-dominated careers.

This imbalance can be changed, however. One's skill set and one's preferences may change also. Take empathy, for example. Once empathy is mastered as product of training and practice, career options expand both in preference and in opportunity, just like mastering the skill of swimming may lead a person to become a lifeguard. If we trained men in the skill of empathy, for example, they might feel more inclined to seek more caregiving jobs.

For men, preference is often a matter of practicality. Men still often take jobs that pay the most because they feel they need to be the primary breadwinner. Author Hanna Rosin noted that 24 of the 25 worst jobs were still nearly all male.[68] Many of these are dangerous positions that justify higher pay. Here, the question can be whether this is preference or social construction or whether it may be a question of preference versus social norms and expectations.

Why anyone makes the career choice they do is a tough question. Organizations need to ferret out this information and understand it if they wish to affect career choices. Imagine how useful it would be to have an onboarding survey that actually asked what factors lead a person to take a job. That would be highly useful information that would help to see the real gender balance picture for an organization. For most organizations, however, understanding the dynamics behind job selection is another example of the complex hurdles an organization can be up against in trying to achieve balance through numbers.

Balancing by numbers is difficult. A number of organizations have tried anything and everything to modify their numbers to no avail. Organizations are up against a long history of perceptions, norms, biases, expectations, and preferences.

Barrier Analysis

Organizations are also up against institutionalized barriers—most often of their own making. There can be any multitude of varied reasons why one sex may shy away from or gravitate to an organization or its offered positions. These could be policies or practices, programs or culture, environment or reputation. At a minimum, organizations should make a practice of doing barrier analysis. This is a structured approach to identifying what hinders a group (men or women, for our purposes) from being adequately represented in or integrated into an organization. It methodology drills down to root causes by asking deeper and deeper "why" questions. There are classes that teach how to conduct a barrier analysis; learning how to do it right it worth every penny. As a barrier identification mechanism and tool of awareness, barrier analysis can be yet another leveling mechanism. I have led a number of barrier analyses and can attest to their usefulness. That said, leadership must fully understand the results of a barrier analysis and be willing to commit to removing hurdles identified.

Ultimately, we are talking about recruiting and retention. Many recruiting strategies can be successful, but what may prove most successful over the long run is encouraging people into nontraditional roles. This has been the linchpin in the movement to get more girls into STEM. The girls in STEM movement can show how to tip the scales successfully. STEM-balancing advocates use a number of approaches that organizations should explore and consider for their own purposes and use. None, however, will be a quick fix. The biggest piece of these types of movements is changing attitudes, which is a matter of promotion and time.

The numbers can be a (partial) fix. Because of its relative difficulty and inconsistent success, however, a numbers-bound strategy is often impractical or unreliable. That is not to say that recruiting is a wasted effort. It is not. Recruiting is a vital piece, an aid to meeting the requirements of balance, and as an aid and tool, it should be used to the extent feasible.

In the end, the goal remains parity in contribution and influence. In constructing anything, there are necessary tools and optional but beneficial tools. The proper wielding of the tools makes things come together successfully. Organizations must take ownership of both tool selection and tool use. As in construction, balance cannot be haphazard. What is being built will support and sustain organizational success—or it won't.

That which is rewarded gets repeated. In the end, if an organization wants to see behaviors that balance, they must be cognizant of and reward such behaviors. Through this, an organization indicates what it truly values. If we reward behaviors that help balance, then more of those behaviors will be exhibited, to the betterment of the organization.

In most organizations women are still casualties of an ineffective and old-fashioned system geared toward the single-income, male breadwinner model. Under that model, what counts are things like diligence, dedication, bold leadership, and others noted previously. What counts gets attention, so performance and performance metrics will get the most attention. Typically, developmental issues receive less credit and attention. These are the very things women may need or excel at. Organizations can benefit from reexamining their metrics and considering what traits and activities they reward. Many organizations need to revise evaluation metrics to include elevating the value of organizational service tasks, such as mentoring new employees. New metrics need to be inserted and owned if the status quo is to change. Levels of bullying, for example, can be measured, publicly reported, and factored into managerial awards. Punitive measures can be taken against employees who turn on other employees.

Not everything that can be done to equalize the numbers was discussed in this chapter. For example, a big issue in hiring and promotion is pure and simple bias and how to overcome it. But my intention here was to focus on non-numbered solutions. There are so many things that can be done to balance the numbers other than simply changing the numbers themselves.

Conclusion

It is true that many pages of this book were dedicated to increasing female presence, voice, contribution, and influence. Solutions to elevate women's contributions and influence were abundantly offered as means of gender balance. But that does not mean men don't have a horse in the race. Study after study has proven that the more women are empowered and the more gender-balanced an organization is, the better the organization or group performs. The most successful organizations are steeped in and excel at programs that give women greater participation and more voice. I would think men would want to be in an organization or work group that excels, because successful organizations benefit everyone involved, men and women alike.

Still, the reality is that women are disadvantaged and undervalued in most organizations. Downward trends in a number of areas continue to disfavor women. At the time of this writing, there are just 28 women CEOs in Fortune 500 companies, down from 32 recently. In 1995, 37% of computer scientists were women. Today, it's 24%. The probability of female students graduating with a bachelor's degree, master's degree, or doctoral degree in science-related fields is 18%, 8%, and 2%, respectively, while the percentages for male students are 37%, 18%, and 6% respectively.

It is not all bad news for women, however. On the plus side, women currently hold 51.4% of managerial and professional jobs. Of the 15 fastest-growing job categories, 12 are occupied primarily by women. Of the 30 professions projected to grow the most, women dominate 20.

As for men, manufacturing has lost 6 million jobs since 2000, while health care and education added about equal that. The share of men in the workforce in 1956 was 98%, in 2012 it was 88%. The trend is particularly pronounced in blue-collar jobs. As the job market shifted from blue-collar positions that required only a high school diploma to more skilled labor, many men fell behind.

The principles of gender balance hold for all, with the goal of ensuring everyone is fully able to contribute.

Aside from jobs, statistics also have something to say concerning the traits exhibited by men and women in recent years. As a possible sign of progress toward a synchronization of traits, meta-analyses show a decrease in male-female differences, such as math and verbal skills.[69] Women increasingly describe themselves with more typically identified male traits, such as being aggressive or taking risks. One of the more important findings of some studies is that women are becoming more confident and men are becoming less so.

In a number of sectors, the skills women have acquired and mastered (e.g., communication, cooperation, negotiation, compromise) are becoming more valuable than the skills men have acquired (e.g., aggression, brawn). There is a direct correlation between the rise in need of feminine skills and the rise in female wages. Male wages are stagnating, while women in some sectors are receiving higher wages and out-earning male counterparts by 43% in some cases. Women now contribute 42.2% of family income, up from 2–6% in 1970.

Statistics don't always tell the full story; observation and experience may say more. I have shared experiences and observations from working with multiple organizations. And here I will share a final story that reflects on the broader societal state of gender.

I gave a presentation on gender balance at the large national American Geophysical Union conference. Walking around the conference center, I naturally took note of the ratio of men and women at this scientific conference and found women were well represented. I also noted and found even more interesting given the professional and scientific nature of the conference, the number of children present, from babies to teens, What I also took note of was that many of these children were with men. They were being cared for by men in numbers nearly equal to those being cared for by women.

Changing social structure includes more shared responsibilities. Women are getting some help from their male partners.

Some signs indicate power is more free-flowing, but parity in contribution and influence in most areas has not been achieved. At that same conference where many men were undertaking childcare responsibilities, a survey of who was actually standing at the lecterns giving presentations showed the program was still vastly dominated by men.

Ultimate judgment on the state of gender, gender relations, and gender issues in the workplace I leave to the reader as a product of observation in their own workplaces.

Inequities do exist in most organizations, and the imbalances hinder the organization, whether or not it is witnessed, recognized, or acknowledged. While an imbalanced ratio of men and women is a major cause and possible solution to these imbalances, I am convinced the fix is not numbers-dependent. More often than not, the numbers are just a means to an end—that end being equitable involvement of men and women to ensure both enjoy inclusion in all processes fully and equitably. What balance really means is parity in contribution and influence. When it comes to achieving organizational gender balance, the scales can be tipped not only by adjusting the numbers of women and men but also by adding more equitable involvement and voice.

An investment in the principles of gender balance delivers organizational and personal rewards. Gender balance is fostered to the betterment of any organization that applies the principles. And while organizational success has been a focus here, that does not mean the individual is not an equal beneficiary. But as it is with everything of value, to get it requires effort—a great deal of organization effort. To begin with, organizational leadership must take ownership of gender balance, acknowledge the issues, and take them head on.

Sadly however, only 66% of companies in corporate America have gender diversity strategies to try to improve these numbers. Globally, it is a mixed bag, with individual governments doing better or worse than others. Large organizations such as the United Nations have strong gender-equality policies and programs but are still finding it an uphill climb of Mount Everest proportions to make global improvements. Such efforts often face daunting cultural pushback.

There is much work yet to be done by organizations—and by you.

Let me end on a personal note. I've always been unhappy with inequality. My path to diversity work actually started as a child. I had a strong sense of being an underdog for a number of reasons. The result was a strong sense of empathy for the undervalued and a strong sense of fairness for all. Even as a kid on the playground, I tried to make the rules so play activity was equitable and inclusive for all. To this day, anything that appears unfair strikes a strong chord with me and gets my attention. In many places, gender disparity is one of those things that strongly resonates as unfair.

I am no longer the kid on the playground making the rules of play. And I can't make the rules of fair play for your organization. I hope, however, that I have given you workable suggestions for solutions. Policies, plans, programs, procedures, and practices can be effective leveling agents. You can use the information and suggestions in this book to fairly and equitably raise individuals and, in turn, raise organizations.

Notes

1. National Center for Education Statistics, 2016.
2. Society of Women Engineers, Research and Trends for Women in STEM web page, http://research.swe.org, accessed July 19, 2019.
3. American Association of University Women, *Barriers and Bias: The Status of Women in Leadership*, 2016.
4. Marcus Noland and Tyler Moran, "Study: Firms with More Women in the C-Suite Are More Profitable," *Harvard Business Review*, February 8, 2016.
5. Credit Suisse, "Large-Cap Companies with at Least One Woman on the Board Have Outperformed Their Peer Group with No Women on the Board by 26% over the Last Six Years, according to a Report by Credit Suisse Research Institute," July 31, 2012, https://www.credit-suisse.com/about-us-news/en/articles/media-releases/42035-201207.html.
6. "Quick Take: Women in Management," Catayst.org, July 2018.
7. "Quick Take: Women in the Workforce—Global," Catayst.org, October 2018.
8. Dina Medland, "Today's Gender Reality in Statistics, or Making Leadership Attractive to Women," Forbes.com, March 7, 2016.
9. US Equal Employment Opportunity Commission, EEOC Women's Work Group Report, EEOC statistics, December 2013.
10. "Scientists Not Immune from Gender Bias, Yale Study Shows," *Yale News*, September 24, 2012.
11. Kieran Snyder, "The Abrasiveness Trap: High-Achieving Men and Women Are Described Differently in Reviews" *Fortune*, August 25, 2014.
12. McKinsey & Co., *Women in the Workplace*, 2017.
13. Kim Parker and Cary Funk, "Gender Discrimination Comes in Many Forms for Today's Working Women," Pew Research Center, December 14, 2017.
14. "Male and Female HR Leaders Are So NOT on the Same Page about Sexism," Fairygodboss, https://fairygodboss.com/articles/male-female-hr-leaders-are-so-not-on-the-same-page-about-sexism.
15. Joan C. Williams, "The 5 Biases Pushing Women out of STEM," *Harvard Business Review*, March 24, 2015.
16. Megan J. Foley, "Patriarchal Killjoys: The Experiences of Three (Women) University Band Directors," PhD diss., Boston College, 2019.
17. Paola Cecchi-Dimeglio, "How Gender Bias Corrupts Performance Reviews, and What to Do about It," *Harvard Business Review*, April 12, 2017.
18. Kieran Snyder, "The Abrasiveness Trap: High-Achieving Men and Women Are Described Differently in Reviews, *Forbes*, August 26, 2014.

19. "Stereotypes Lower Math Performance in Women, but Effects Go Unrecognized, IU Study Finds," Indiana University Bloomington press release, March 26, 2015.

20. "Women Matter 2: Female Leadership, a Competitive Edge for the Future," McKinsey and Company, 2008.

21. Linda Babcock and Sara Laschever, *Women Don't Ask: Negotiation and the Gender Divide* (Princeton, NJ: Princeton University Press, 2003).

22. Linda Babcock and Sara Laschever, *Women Don't Ask: Negotiation and the Gender Divide* (Princeton, NJ: Princeton University Press, 2003).

23. Kay Bussey and Albert Bandura, "Social Cognitive Theory of Gender Development and Differentiation," *Psychological Review* 106, no. 4 (1999): 676–713.

24. Candace West and Don H. Zimmerman, "Doing Gender," *Gender and Society* 1, no. 2 (1987): 125–151.

25. David M. Mayer, "How Men Get Penalized for Straying from Masculine Norms," *Harvard Business Review*, October 8, 2018.

26. David M. Mayer, "How Men Get Penalized for Straying from Masculine Norms," *Harvard Business Review*, October 8, 2018.

27. Tom Y. Chang and Agne Kajackaite, "Battle for the Thermostat: Gender and the Effect of Temperature on Cognitive Performance," *PLoS One* 14, no. 5 (2019): e0216362.

28. McKinsey, *Women in the Workplace*, 2016.

29. Amy C. Waninger, *Network beyond Bias: Making Diversity a Competitive Advantage for Your Career* (CreateSpace, 2018).

30. Tonja Jacobi and Dylan Schweers, "Justice, Interrupted: The Effect of Gender, Ideology, and Seniority at Supreme Court Oral Arguments," *Virginia Law Review* 103 (2017): 1379; Northwestern Law and Econ Research Paper 17-03.

31. Megan J. Foley, "Patriarchal Killjoys: The Experiences of Three (Women) University Band Directors," PhD diss., Boston College, 2019.

32. Anita Woolley and Thomas W. Malone, "Defend Your Research: What Makes a Team Smarter? More Women," *Harvard Business Review*, June 2011.

33. Leslie Bradshaw, "Why Women having a Seat at the Table Is Not Enough," Forbes.com, August 4, 2011.

34. "Engaging Men in Gender Initiatives: What Change Agents Need to Know," Catalyst, 2009.

35. "Engaging Men in Gender Initiatives: What Change Agents Need to Know," Catalyst, 2009.

36. "Women in the Workplace," McKinsey and Company and Lean In, 2018.

37. Paolo Gaudiano and Ellen Hunt, "Advertising Week Survey: Men and Women Have Different Perceptions about Gender Bias," *Forbes*, September 26, 2016.

38. "Women in the Workplace," McKinsey and Company and Lean In, 2018.

39. Claire Atkinson, "What Happens When There Are More Women than Men in the Boardroom?" NBC News, June 6, 2019.

40. "Better Together: Increasing Male Engagement in Gender Equality Efforts in Australia," Chief Executive Women and Bain and Company, 2019.

41. (2018 New York Post, NPR [National Public Radio]).

42. *The Facts Behind the #MeToo Movement: A National Study on Sexual Harassment and Assault* (Reston, VA: Stop Street Harassment, 2018).

43. Joshua A. Krisch, "Are Most Men Sexist? The Data Says Yes Even If They Say No," Fatherly.com, December 24, 2018.

44. "Report of the Co-chairs of the EEOC Select Task Force on the Study of Harassment in the Workplace," US Equal Employment Opportunity Commission, June 2016.

45. Lisa Heap, "Hear My Voice: The Experiences of Victorian Women at Work," Library Fellowship Paper 2, Parliamentary Library and Information Service, Parliament of Victoria (Australia).

46. Michael Alison Chandler, "Men Account for Nearly 1 in 5 Complaints of Workplace Sexual Harassment with the EEOC," *Washington Post*, April 8, 2018.

47. Maeve Duggan, "Online Harassment 2017," Pew Research Center, July 11, 2017.

48. National Academies of Sciences, Engineering, and Medicine, *Sexual Harassment of Women: Climate, Culture, and Consequences in Academic Sciences, Engineering, and Medicine* (Washington, DC: National Academies Press, 2018).

49. Heather McLaughlin, Christopher Uggin, and Amy Blackstone, "The Cost of Sexual Harassment," Gender and Society, June 7, 2017.

50. Kate Klunk, "Disclosing Sexual Harassment in the Workplace," *York Daily Record*, April 23, 2019.

51. Lisa Heap, "Women Don't Speak up over Workplace Harassment Because No One Hears Them if They Do," Phys.org, December 14, 2018.

52. "Sexual Harassment in the Spotlight," Media, Entertainment, and Arts Alliance, https://www.meaa.org/campaigns/sexual-harassment-in-the-spotlight.

53. Lisa Heap, "Women Don't Speak Up over Workplace Harassment Because No One Hears Them if They Do," Phys.org, December 14, 2018.

54. Peter Glick and Susan T. Fiske, "Ambivalent Sexism Revisited," *Psychology of Women Quarterly* 35, no. 3 (2011): 530–535.

55. Tara Golshan, "Study Finds 75 Percent of Workplace Harassment Victims Experienced Retaliation When They Spoke Up," Vox, October 15, 2017.

56. Onyi Lam, Brian Broderick, Stefan Wojcik, and Adam Hughes, "Gender and Jobs in Online Image Searches," Pew Research Center, December 17, 2018.

57. Michael D. Matthews, "The 3 C's of Trust," *Psychology Today*, May 3, 2016.

58. Jack Zenger and Joseph Folkman, "Are Women Better Leaders than Men?" *Harvard Business Review*, March 15, 2012.

59. Valerie Bolden-Barrett, "Gallup: Women Tend to Be More Engaged at Work," HR Dive, November 18, 2016.

60. Michael Casey, "When Competing in a Male-Dominated Field, Women Should 'Man Up,'" *Fortune*, August 14, 2014.

61. Michael Casey, "When Competing in a Male-Dominated Field, Women Should 'Man Up,'" *Fortune*, August 14, 2014.

62. Jessica Miller-Merrell, "Women Working with Other Women: How to Support One Another," Workology.com, April 11, 2018.

63. Shelley Zalis, "Power of the Pack: Women Who Support Women Are More Successful," Forbes, March 6, 2019.

64. Rachna Baruah, "This Women's Day, Focus on Gender-Equality at Workplace," Entrepreneur India, March 8, 2019.

65. Margie Warrell, "Mentoring Matters: How More Women Can Get the Right People in Their Corner," *Forbes*, June 24, 2017.

66. "Engaging Men in Gender Initiatives: What Change Agents Need to Know," Catalyst, 2009.

67. Robin J. Ely, "The Power in Demography: Women's Social Constructions of Gender Identity at Work," *Academy of Management Journal* 38, no. 3 (1995): 589–634.

68. Hanna Rosin, *The End of Men: And the Rise of Women* (New York: Riverhead Books, 2012).

69. J. S. Hyde, E. Fennema, and S. J. Lamon, "Gender Differences in Mathematics Performance: A Meta-Analysis," *Psychological Bulletin* 107, no. 2 (1990): 139–155.

About the Author

David Rowell is a lifelong professional facilitator, instructor, consultant, and author. For many years he was an instructor for multiple US federal agencies, where he taught leadership, team-building, and women's leadership across the United States and internationally.

As the founder of Parity Consulting, David continues his work in these areas for both public and private organizations. He has worked closely with large international organizations in promotion of gender mainstreaming and gender equality principles. David's efforts focus on organizational gender balance. This subject addresses the negative organizational impacts of gender imbalance and the positive organizational impacts of gender balance. He is a strong advocate for gender relations in the workplace, a strong champion of women, and a staunch supporter of both women and men working together in supportive partnership.

David also presents on behalf of the National Diversity Council and is an associate consultant for Fowlkes Consulting, a leading global firm that specializes in LGBTQ+ issues. Of the latter, as a speaker, trainer, and consultant, David specializes in transgender issues.

David is a sought-after blogger on the topics of gender, LGBTQ+ issues, diversity, and leadership.

Email: parityconsultant@gmail.com
Web: paritycf.com
Facebook: http://www.facebook.com/parityconsultant/
Twitter: https://twitter.com/parityconsulta

www.ingramcontent.com/pod-product-compliance
Lightning Source LLC
Chambersburg PA
CBHW071534220526
45469CB00003B/770